中青年经济与管理学者文库

本书出版受到中南财经政法大学青年教师创新研究专项资助,项目编号:2722021BX004。

近代银行业同业关系与经营绩效研究

Research on Interbank Relationship and
Economic Performance of Modern Banking
Industry during the Republican Era

孔令宇 著

中国财经出版传媒集团
中国财政经济出版社

图书在版编目（CIP）数据

近代银行业同业关系与经营绩效研究／孔令宇著．
--北京：中国财政经济出版社，2021.5
（中青年经济与管理学者文库）
ISBN 978-7-5223-0473-1

Ⅰ.①近… Ⅱ.①孔… Ⅲ.①银行业-研究-中国-近代 Ⅳ.①F832.95

中国版本图书馆 CIP 数据核字（2021）第 057659 号

责任编辑：孙　琛　　　　　责任印制：党　辉
封面设计：智点创意　　　　责任校对：胡永立

近代银行业同业关系与经营绩效研究
JINDAI YINHANGYE TONGYE GUANXI YU JINGYING JIXIAO YANJIU

中国财政经济出版社 出版

URL：http：//www.cfeph.cn
E-mail：cfeph@cfeph.cn
（版权所有　翻印必究）
社址：北京市海淀区阜成路甲 28 号　邮政编码：100142
营销中心电话：010-88191522
天猫网店：中国财政经济出版社旗舰店
网址：https：//zgczjjcbs.tmall.com
北京财经印刷厂印刷　各地新华书店经销
成品尺寸：148mm×210mm　32 开　8.375 印张　200 000 字
2021 年 5 月第 1 版　2021 年 5 月北京第 1 次印刷
定价：40.00 元
ISBN 978-7-5223-0473-1
（图书出现印装问题，本社负责调换，电话：010-88190548）
本社质量投诉电话：010-88190744
打击盗版举报热线：010-88191661　QQ：2242791300

本书的出版受到中南财经政法大学学科建设统筹项目的资助,项目编号:XKHJ202127。

本书前期材料、数据的整理和分析受到中南财经政法大学中央财政专项的资助。

策划人语

题记：一个人的精神成长史，取决于他的阅读史。只有阅读能最有效地培养精神生活习惯，而好的习惯又培养性格，性格决定人生。

——我们自豪，因为我们就是创造这精神产品的人。

选择了飞翔，总能看到蓝天；选择了远航，总能感受大海。人生不仅要作出选择，也要坚持住自己的选择。学会计、当编辑是我的意外选择。人说编辑是为人作嫁，可是这一选择我坚持了27年，苦在其中，乐在其中，也算是有声有色。每当我把一本本好书呈献给人们的时候，我觉得我是"富贵"的人：富，不是你身上的钱财，而是你心里的满足；贵，不是你地位的显赫，而是你被人需要的程度。

书海探寻，情怀永恒

我要说，做编辑我幸运，因为我不仅是第一个读者，可以对作品"品头论足"，也可以对作品"生杀予夺"；更重要的是，这是一个很高层次的平台，在多年与名家的交往和名著的"对话"中，深深地为他们的人格和才学所感动，被作品的精彩所吸引，这不仅使我"下笔如有神"，更使我的思想和灵魂也受到一次次洗礼和震撼，得到一次次升华。对于我的作者我的书，如数家珍，作者中不乏才学和为人同样过人的多位泰斗和"颜值高责任大"的众多才子佳人；策划的作品不仅立足专业还兼顾人文，也是情怀所在，专业加人文路才会更宽。

多年的体会是，作为一名编辑，起码要"三心二意"，即"责任心、细心、耐心"和"服务意识、创新意识"。要多策划一些有分量的拳头产品，用一个选题推动一个系统工程，用一个系统工程培养一个出版社品牌。给新入职编辑讲座时我做过一个比喻：编辑两项基本功，审稿——甚至要比博导审批学生论文还要全面、细致；选题策划——要像电影导演一样做"星探"，善于发现优秀作者和挖掘好的原创作品。记不得 27 年来我策划和编辑了多少书，组织和策划了一大批教材、业务培训用书、通俗读物、理论专著等，有的获得过国家、省部级各类奖项，有的以其填补空白、社会热点、风格新颖、开拓尝试等特点受到读者的欢迎。20 世纪 90 年代我开始自主策划选题，多年来每年都有新丛书问世。比如，21 世纪初内部控制研究在国内刚兴起时，策划了《现代内部控制丛书》，其中的《企业内部控制管理操作手册》是我鼓励作者将自己饱含心血的经过长期钻研和实践并被证明有效的成果奉献付梓，使更多的人能受益于此，这无疑是对我国内部控制理论探索和实践发展的一种贡献，而内部控制选题至今还是热点。2013 年的《来去无尘——一位财政部长的生前事》所展现的吴波精神,与深入推进党风廉政建设相得益彰,得到中央领导同志的高度重视和重要批示。中央各大主流媒体纷纷连续报道,掀起了全社会学习吴波高尚情操的热潮。2014年至今的前沿选题《财务云丛书》等也越来越受到业界认可。

想是问题,做是答案

众所周知,目前的图书出版业在行业竞争和纸质图书受到严重冲击的情况下,出版人无不感到莫大的危机。在这种背景下,策划一套专业图书是颇感困惑的一件事,风险更大。但即使这样我们也不能因噎废食、停滞不前,还要积极应对,继续发挥纸质图书的固有特质,挖掘出版内容和形式都精彩的原创作品,适应新形势下读者的更高需求。2017年,我们接受新的挑战,开启新的征程,又策划了《中青年经济与管理学者文库》《当代税收名家丛书》《中国税务律师系列丛书》《现代管理实务丛书》《高等院校应用型会计人才精细化培养系列教材》等,继续为扶持学术研究和总结最新成果,在高端研究与专业知识普及和应用之间搭建一座座有益的桥梁。

每一个时代的经济环境不同,理论研究和实务探索所需要解决的问题也有所差别。当前我国不仅处于经济结构调整和供给侧改革的攻坚期,同时也处于大数据和互联网突飞猛进的变革期,矛盾叠加,风险交汇,市场环境和组织模式不断演变发展、推陈出新,经济、管理、财税等领域的新理论、新思想、新方法、新工具也层出不穷。乱花渐欲迷人眼,击水三千浪几何?这些领域的研究人员被时代赋予了更艰巨的责任,也面临着更高、更多元的要求,我们不仅要具备更广阔的学术视野,而且要有更严谨的学术思维。

输在犹豫,赢在行动

《中青年经济与管理学者文库》的作者,都是我国经济与管理领域的中坚力量,也是未来的大家。他们中有些人潜心从事理论研究,有些人则深耕在实务一线,但无论现实身份如何,视野全都没有被拘泥在"象牙塔"内。他们从不同视角对市场经济的不同要素进行细致审视,然后汇聚于"财经版"这面旗帜之下,相互碰撞,彼此激荡,力求在市场经济转型升级的关键时期留下最新鲜的"中国印记"。

这些经济与管理领域的中青年学者,就是我国市场经济发展的潜力与优势,他们的研究成果,不仅将引领市场经济的各个组成环节向更科学、更先进的方向发展,而且将成为我国政府和企业在未来经济世界扮演更重要角色的支点与动力。祝愿这些中青年学者能攀上更高的学术之山,走向更远的研究之路,也期待宏观、中观、微观各个层面的市场参与者都能从这套文库中得到切实的启发与指引,在全面深化改革、增强发展活力的关键时期,发挥正能量和积极作用,为经济社会发展增添新的动力!

如果您认可,如果您有意愿,欢迎您和您的朋友加盟我们的作者队伍!在中国财经出版传媒集团的"旗舰"下,中国财政经济出版社这"老字号",一定励精图治,谱写新的篇章。我们用"龙的精神,玉的品质"来助力您实现梦想!

策划人:樊清玉

邮箱:qingyuf@ sina. com

2017 年春

Preface

This book examines three themes that focus on inter – banking connections and their impacts on modern banking development in the 1930s.

Chapter 2 provides an overview of the modern bank sector and highlights the inter – banking relations. I find that it was characterized by a strong network of interlocking directorates by tracing the shape, structure, and development of links within the sector. This network shows a dominating central cluster, indicating that the sector was characterized by internal cooperation rather than competition. Similarly, new entrants were usually linked to existing banks, indicating that entry was driven by the expansion of existing banks rather than the rise of new competition. Finally, central locations of public banks within the cluster indicate that the government gained influence over the sector through direct bank ownership.

Chapter 3 investigates how board connections in an inter-bank network affect their corporate policy decisions. I find evidence that corporate decisions of banks are influenced by their social peers, namely the more directors two banks share with each other, the more similar are their corporate strategies. Also, banks with a central position in the boardroom network make corporate decisions less distinctively. Additionally, the empirical outcomes show that co-moved corporate policies are mainly driven by banks' intentions to pursue profits and eliminate risks, known as profitability and insurance effects.

I further examine whether inter-banking connections based on interlocking directorates contributed to the overall performance in Chapter 4. I find characteristics of banks, which share directors with other banks, are significantly different compared to those of unconnected counterparts. The empirical results elucidate a high positive correlation between banks' profitability and their connections with rivals through interlocking directors.

Last but not least, Chapter 5 investigates the development of the interlocking directorate network between domestic Chinese banks from 1933 to 1936 to understand how financial institutions structure cooperation within the sector in response to uncertain external environments and weak property rights. This part uses a dynamic network simulation approach to address the reflection problem between bank performance and network formation, illuminating the factors driving the network evolution and shaping the structure of cooperation between Chinese banks.

Contents

Chapter 1 Introduction .... (1)

Chapter 2 The Banking Networks: An Overview ...... (10)
  2.1 Introduction .... (11)
  2.2 Historical Environment of China in 20th Century .... (14)
  2.3 The Modern Chinese Banking Industry During the Nanjing Decade .... (20)
  2.4 Links and Networks .... (27)
  2.5 Connections and Cooperation .... (36)
  2.6 Government and Banking Cooperation .... (55)
  2.7 Conclusion .... (61)

Chapter 3 Corporate Policies Propagation Through Board Connection .... (63)
  3.1 Introduction .... (64)
  3.2 Background .... (74)

3.3　Data and Variables ……………………………（81）
3.4　The Impact of Inter-bank Ties on
　　　Corporate Policy …………………………………（95）
3.5　Endogeneity and Further Tests ………………（109）
3.6　Bank Network and Operational Policies …………（123）
3.7　Why did Banks Coordinate Their
　　　Corporate Policy? …………………………………（131）
3.8　Conclusion …………………………………………（142）

Chapter 4　Connections and Performance: The Impact of
　　　　　　Interlocking Directorates ……………………（144）
4.1　Introduction ………………………………………（145）
4.2　Historical Background …………………………（150）
4.3　The Relationship Between Board-connectedness
　　　and Performance …………………………………（156）
4.4　Robustness and Further Tests …………………（171）
4.5　Conclusion …………………………………………（186）

Chapter 5　The Evolution of the Interlocking
　　　　　　Directorate Network ……………………………（188）
5.1　Introduction ………………………………………（189）
5.2　Bank Network and Characteristics ……………（193）
5.3　Mechanisms and Simulations …………………（199）
5.4　Results ……………………………………………（215）
5.5　Conclusion …………………………………………（222）

Chapter 6　Conclusion ……………………………………（224）

Appendix A　Additional Information on Chapter 3 ······ (227)
　A. 1　Definitions of Variables ································ (227)
　A. 2　Network Centrality Measures ·························· (230)
　A. 3　Data Sample on Bank Boards, Directors
　　　　and Balance Sheets ····································· (231)

Appendix B　Additional Information on Chapter 4 ······ (235)
　B. 1　Variable Definitions ····································· (235)
　B. 2　Network Centrality Measures ·························· (236)
　B. 3　Representing and Measuring Networks ············· (238)
　B. 4　A Propensity – Score Matching (PSM) Analysis
　　　　of the Difference in Performance Between
　　　　Connected and Isolated Banks ······················· (239)

References ··· (241)

Introduction

Chinese modern banks, so modern – style banks modeled on Western practices (for example corporations of limited liability, relative impersonal relationships with customers, and mortgage loans)①, achieved in the face of extreme political and economic turbulence, and produced significant results by the outbreak of the Japanese War of Aggression against China in 1937. The literature documents that interlocking directorates, key characteristics in the sector, were widespread, i. e. directors sharing by multiple banks featured

---

① The foreign banks refer to the institutions which handle money and financial business along the line of Western business methods in China. In 1848 a British – chartered Oriental Banking Corporation opened its premises in Shanghai, which was considered as the beginning of the banking expansion in China. By 1937 the British group led the foreign money market, with the old Mercantile Bank of India and the Chartered Bank of India, Australia and China as well as the prominent Hongkong and Shanghai Banking Corporation (HSBC).

prominently (Lan 2014; Cheng 2003; Sheehan 2005)[①]. The interlocking director relationships formed explicit connections among institutions, potentially creating an inter - bank social network with nodes represent the financial institutions and ties symbolize the director - sharing among banks. Within the network, a set of nodes (i. e. banks) are connected with ties, which indicate the links among banks when directors are shared by them. It could exert considerable impacts on agents' (i. e. individual banks) policy decision making and economic performance according to the social network paradigm in organization research[②]. However, it lacks both systematic and quantitative examinations on the consequences of these board connections, and implications for economic and business development. A number of questions remain unanswered or controversial, including what shape did the social networks take, were such connections important for firms' operation, and how did networks evolve in general in response to unstable external environments?

The aim of the study is to establish an inter - banking social network based on Chinese bank interlocking directorates, and carry on a systematic analysis of the inter - bank board connections using aspects of network theory. Using aspects of network theory for an examination of inter - organizational networks is a tested method. A

[①] For example, Sheehan (2005) provides a statistics in 1936 regarding the director - sharing in the Chinese modern banking sector, showing that of the 122 banks in his sample, 80.3% had at least one interlocking director on their boards, leaving only 24 banks as independent isolates.

[②] For a comprehensive review of the inter - organizational network paradigm, see Borgatti and Foster (2003).

Chapter 1 Introduction

voluminous literature, both from theoretical and empirical aspects, have demonstrated the value in engaging in this sort of analysis and the opportunity it provides to isolate network implications and distinctive trends. Although a consensus on what resources or influence of network ties, i. e., the interlocking relations among banks in our context, might convey, recent studies have shifted toward an informational perspective that sees interlocks as a conduit in which organizations reduce uncertainties and share information about acceptable and effective corporate practices (Borgatti and Foster 2003; Shropshire 2010). For example, empirical works include the corporate acquisition behavior (Rousseau and Stroup 2015), the adoption of accounting practices and earnings management contagion (Kang 2008; Chiu, Teoh, and Tian 2013), the option backdating (Bizjak, Lemmon, and Whitby 2009), and innovations (Helmers, Patnam, and Rau 2017).

The social network in the China context, based on what is called guanxi (social connections), lies at the heart of economic, social and political life. Guanxi essentially works as a substitute for formal institutional support (Xin and Pearce 1996). Although contemporary study on Chinese business suggests guanxi – oriented society does not necessarily imply a densely interlocked business network (Ren, Au, and Birch 2009), modern banking in the 1930s featured shared professional values based on common attributes of bankers, such as native place, classmate, and kinship (Bergere 1989), that leads to a prevalence of interlocking directorates (Lan 2014, p. 171).

I therefore initially provide an overview of the banking networks during the Chinese Republican era (1928 – 1937) and the Great

3

Depression that presented an environment characterized by economic and political uncertainty and weak property rights. Chapter 2 traces the shape, structure, and development of links within the sector and shows that the interlocking directorate network had a dominating central cluster, indicating that the sector was characterized by internal cooperation rather than competition. Similarly, new entrants were usually linked to existing banks, indicating that entry was driven by the expansion of existing banks rather than the rise of new competition. Finally, it demonstrates the central locations of public banks within the cluster, arguing that the status indicates that the government gained influence over the sector by linking public banks with private banks throughout the whole sector. This chapter shows that the domestic financial sector reacted successfully to the threats of the external environment by weaving a close web of interdependence, including with the government.

Next, interlocking theory in management predicts a similarity in organizational behavior (Mizruchi 1989). For instance, Westphal, Seidel, and Stewart (2001) highlight that interlock ties facilitate firms' imitation of decision process, and recent corporate finance studies suggest that the existence of shared directors has a deep impact on firms' corporate behavior[①]. According to the logic, I explore how board connections in an inter-bank network affect a bank's corporate policy decisions in Chapter 3.

---

① A voluminous literature in finance highlights that social connections at board level can serve as a conduit by which information is communicated or resources are exchanged, for instance, Larcker, So, and Wang (2013), Hochberg, Ljungqvist, and Lu (2007), Fracassi (2017), and Faleye, Kovacs, and Venkateswaran (2014).

Specifically, I establish bank networks between domestic Chinese banks based on interlocking directorates for the year 1933 to year 1936, and find evidence that corporate decisions of banks were influenced by their social peers, in other words, the more directors two banks shared with each other, the more similar were their corporate strategies. The analysis also reveals that peer behavior affected a bank's own decisions not only bilaterally but network – wide. Banks with a central position in the boardroom network made corporate decisions less idiosyncratically and more in line with the whole sector.

I then investigate why banks coordinated their corporate policy through interlocking directorates. The examination comes to two important points about underlying reasons. First, I find positive and significant relationships between a number of policy measures and banks' economic performance motivating corporate policy co – movement among bank pairs—that modern Chinese banks coordinated or imitated the bond/cash/reserve related corporate policies of their peers to achieve better performance, which I call the profitability effect of board ties. Second, I introduce an empirical model that compares the excess fluctuations of banks' profitability between banks with more board connections and those with fewer links. The result shows that more board connections led to fewer fluctuations in profitability, suggesting that such connections were associated with banks' intentions to seek assurance and reduce risk. Overall, the findings support the view that banks cooperated intimately with each other at board level and interlocking directorates were critical channels for strategical choices and strategies in the 1930s.

Economists have long been interested in the impact of director sharing on firms' economic performance. A natural extension of the policy co-movement across bank pairs is to examine whether these inter-banking connections contributed to the overall performance of these modern Chinese banks. In Chapter 4, I, therefore, provide a comprehensive examination of the relationship between inter-bank links and economic performance.

The chapter uses four centrality measures, which are *degree*, *closeness*, *betweenness*, and *eigenvector centrality*, derived from social network analysis (SNA) to capture individual banks' position and extent of connectedness in the boardroom network. The annual interbank networks from 1933 to 1936, which are used in the empirical analysis, are based on the board compositions of 209 Chinese banks involving 3060 individuals collected from the Bank Annual (1934–1937), an official record of annual financial statistics, also the main source for the bank accounting data used.

The empirical analysis highlights ambiguous results. Closeness centrality was statistically correlated with banks' performance, for both return on assets and profit per staff member. In contrast, I find no significant relationship between network location and the performance of banks once I replace *closeness centrality* with *degree*, *betweenness* and *eigenvector centrality* as alternative network position indicators. The outcome of the analysis suggests that *closeness* significantly differed from other indicators in measuring individual banks' position, indicating that it carried different centrality information compared to other measures and reflected a more relevant linkage effect than the other network indicators in this historical

Chapter 1 Introduction

Chinese context.

The empirical outcome offers evidence that banks, that were located more centrally as measured by a higher value of closeness centrality, exhibited better financial performance. Economically, my results imply that banks with relatively closer links to outside boards throughout the whole sector achieved a better performance, possibly linked to more and better exchange of information and in particular operational and management know – how.

Chapter 5 pays attention to the evolution of the interlocking directorate network in general. I investigate the development of the interlocking directorate network between domestic Chinese banks from the year 1933 to year 1936 to understand how financial institutions structure cooperation within the sector in response to unstable external environments and weak property rights. This chapter uses a dynamic network simulation approach to address the inflection problem between bank performance and network formation, illuminating what factors underlay the network evolution and shaped the structure of cooperation between Chinese banks.

The evolution of the network is analyzed with a Stochastic Actor – oriented Network model, the SIENA methodology. This approach specifies an objective function for each actor and bank, consisting of a set of mechanisms. Each mechanism models a particular factor that potentially could affect the formation or dissolution of particular ties. The estimation then simulates the evolution of the model using this objective function and derives a parameter value for each mechanism in comparison with the actual observed network evolution data, including the statistical significance of these parameters. I draw these mechanisms based on the network structure itself, financial, operational and other bank characteristics.

The empirical results demonstrate that network effects existed, with a tendency to form triads and a decentralization effect due to a negative effect of the existing number of ties. A number of operational effects mattered, including the types and ages of two potential partner banks. Similarly, financial characteristics mattered, in particular, the relative ratio of two banks' assets, while size on its own did not have an effect. The involvement of national public banks[①] mattered, with the pattern showing a strong swing from positive to negative effect with the 1935 financial reforms. Finally, the bank's financial performance, its levels of RoE (return on equity) and RoE (return on equity) growth, mattered for its tendency to expand its interlocking directorate network.

The analysis further explores the issue of endogeneity through including RoE as another outcome measure, therefore simulating the evolution of both outcomes in the same model. While this additional analysis confirms the results found in the network, the only estimation they do not lend support the impact of interlocking directorates on the financial performance of the banks. Potential explanations for this result, in particular constraints of the simulation approach, are discussed.

In summary, the thesis stresses the importance, effects,

---

① The national public banks, i.e. the central banking group, were performed by a group of four public banks by 1937, namely the Central bank of China, the Bank of China, the Bank of Communications and the Farmers Bank of China.

implications, and development of Chinese banking networks during the Republican Era. As outlined, the book is organized into four parts followed by a conclusion. In Chapter 2, I provide an overview and background of Chinese banking and the business networks. Chapter 3 discusses corporate policy contagion through the network of interlocking directorates. In Chapter 4, I investigate the relationship between the centrality of banks within the interlocking directorate network and economic performance. Chapter 5 carries out an analysis of the drivers of the evolution and adjustment of the network itself, and finally, Chapter 6 concludes the contributions of my work.

The Banking Networks: An Overview

The Chinese Republican era, in particular also during the Great Depression, presented an environment characterized by economic and political uncertainty and weak property rights. Nevertheless I document that the domestic Chinese banking sector flourished during this time. I find that it was characterized by a strong network of interlocking directorates by tracing the shape, structure and development of links within the sector. This network shows a dominating central cluster, indicating that the sector was characterized by internal cooperation rather than competition. Similarly, new entrants were usually linked to existing banks, indicating that entry was driven by the expansion of existing banks rather than the rise of new competition. Finally, central locations of public banks within the cluster indicate that the government gained influence over the sector through direct bank ownership. This paper shows that the domestic financial sector reacted successfully to the threats of the external environment by weaving a close web of interdependence, including that with the government.

2.1 Introduction

Around the fall of the Chinese Empire, the financial sector in China was split between traditional, domestic financial institutions and international banks. By the outbreak of the Japanese War of Aggression against China in 1937 domestic Chinese banks patterned on Western counterparts had risen to dominance over the domestic business comparing to its counterparts (Cheng 2003, p.75). These new financial institutions emerged in an external environment of political uncertainty, weak property rights and limited governmental reach, which obviously influenced the internal structure of this rapidly developing industry. This paper focuses on one central aspect of the sector's response, namely the extent of cooperation, as well as competition, between its banks. How did they relate to each other while facing external uncertainty and a weak government?

Cooperation and links between firms, and in particular banks, have been a topic for economic and financial historians. One important approach to measure formal relationships is to focus on explicit links created by common personnel. Directors and managers might work for multiple firms, which link them together through an interlocking directorate. Such relationships have been shown to influence multiple aspects of involved firms, from access to capital to formal cooperations and even mergers①.

While most analyses focus on the effects that such a link has on individual firms, another viewpoint is to see that link as one edge of a network formed between the firms in the sector. This opens up the utilization of tools developed by Social Network Analysis to describe and understand the internal structure of an industry such as the domestic Chinese banking sector, which is build on Sheehan (2005), who uses basic cross – sectional network statistics to demonstrate that the traditional focus of the literature on the influence of cliques is too small and therefore a wider, modern business focused approach is more appropriate. Consequently, I take this up and construct the network of interlocking directorate between relevant banks for the year 1933 to year 1936, a period forms the end of the Nanjing era, the final decade of the Chinese Republic leading up to the World War II on a global scale.

Section 2 provides the historical background of China's political development for the time period from the fall of the Empire to the Warlord era ending in the Nanjing decade. I also provide additional details about the development of the financial sector at large, which leads into section 3 and a deeper look into these new modern Chinese banks and their rise over this time period. This includes a categorization into different business models, public and private

---

① Mizruchi (1996) provides a nice analysis framework over interlock directorates and the economic implications in early times. More recently, a voluminous literature stress the inter – firm relations on firms behavior and economics outcomes, for example, Fracassi (2017), Dass et al. (2014), Larcker, So, and Wang (2013), and Helmers, Patnam, and Rau (2017).

Chapter 2   The Banking Networks: An Overview

ownership, and the geographic distribution of their headquarters.

The technical and methodological background for the network analysis is outlined in section 4, which provides also more details about the interlocking directorates that form the network. This includes the reasons and motivations for firms in general and Chinese banks in particular to institutionalize their relationships with each other in this way. The section also provides more information about the construction of the network, in particular the data for and definition of interlocking directorates used in the analysis, setting the stage for applying network analysis tools.

The initial analysis of the annual networks reveals that the sector was characterized by a dominant core cluster and a number of essentially unconnected banks. Section 5 demonstrates this indication of a high level of cooperation in the sector in detail and then focuses on the characteristics of the core cluster, revealing more aspects of the cooperation between the banks. Based on different centrality measures from Social Network Analysis, I argue that although larger banks were at the center of this cluster, banks at the periphery also formed a dense network of interlocking directorates with each other, reducing the dependency on dominant, central institutions. The link patterns of relatively young institutions also show a surprisingly large number of connections, indicating that new entrants reflected expansionary motives of existing banks rather than new competitors.

Analyzing the characteristics of this core cluster shows also the participation of publicly owned banks. Section 6 traces the governments involvement in the sector and argues that the relationships of public banks with private banks in the sector were the main control mechanism the government had to influence the sector and monetary arrangements at large.

2.2 Historical Environment of China in 20th Century

2.2.1 China in the early 20th century: historical background

The period from year 1900 to year 1937 straddles several sub-periods of a tumultuous era in modern Chinese history. In the wake of a heavy defeat by the Japanese navy in year 1895, the Chinese Qing Dynasty empire started on a path towards constitutional reform. Efforts were directly modeled on Japan's thorough Meiji reforms. Constitutional reforms covered broad aspects of government affairs including education, with the adoption of a Western-style schooling system and the end of the traditional imperial examination scheme, and the legal system with a new code and judicial system. Importantly, the so-called "New Policies" recognized the central role of the private sector for a market economy and paved the way for the introduction of property rights that contradicted the traditional philosophy about property, which could be summarized as: Kings have long arms. All the lands and people belong to the emperor. However, these reform efforts were short-lived and collapsed with the end of the empire in 1911[1].

---

[1] For a comprehensive interpretation of the late Qing Dynasty, see Fairbank (1978) and Fairbank and Liu (1980).

Chapter 2 The Banking Networks: An Overview

From the fall of the Qing Dynasty in 1911 onwards, China was caught in a situation of internal strife during the era of the Beijing or Northern regime (year 1911 - year 1928). During this time span, the country was divided among former military cliques of Qing Army and various regional factions. The era was characterized by constant clashes and multiple military conflicts between varying alliances of these groups[1].

Although the Beijing government was nominally considered to be the central government, actual political power was widely dispersed among local regimes and warlords. Consequently, its influence over local affairs was severely limited, including in law enforcement and commercial regulations.

In September 1926, the armies of the Chinese Nationalists, the Kuomintang (KMT), marched into the central Yangzi region, opening their "Northern Expedition" that saw them prevail militarily over most opposing forces. By the end of year 1928, the KMT had successfully united China. Although resistance initially remained, in particular it flared up with the Central Plains War of 1930, the unification marked the beginning of the Nanjing decade (year 1928 - year 1937), The era came to an end in year 1937. China's political unification under the Nationalist government provided the modern Chinese economy with a more stable environment for its development, resulting in rapid modernization in urban areas during these years.

Internationally, the emergence of a unified China coincided with

---

[1] Bonavia (1995) details the warlords and political cliques during the post - Qing era.

the advent of the Great Depression. Although its international exposure was limited, China was not fully immune to the ramifications. One important difference was that China's monetary system was based on silver in contrast to the generally prevailing gold standard. Consequently, China's initial experience differed, in particular it did not experience a massive price drop in the first years (Shiroyama 2008, p. 2 – p. 3).

In 1934, however, the US government approved a silver purchase agreement, known as the Silver Purchase Act, which led to an increase in silver production in the United States and a rise in global silver prices. It had a significant impact on China both socially and economically, as China's currency system was on the silver basis. For instance, credit contractions eliminated firms borrowing from banks, which increased labor unrest and Communist Party penetration among their workers (Braggion, Manconi, and Zhu 2018). Chinese exports suffered and the simultaneous deflation affected domestic industries as well. In order to shield the economy from the negative effects of silver price fluctuations, the KMT government implemented a new currency policy, the "Fabi" reform, on November 4th, 1935. It abandoned the silver backing of the Yuan and declared notes issued by four publicly owned banks to be the only legal tender. That former governments had left the management of silver to private smelting shops and further monetary arrangement to private markets marks the first time in Chinese history that the central government asserted direct control over the national money supply. These reforms also marked the end of the free banking era and the start of a more active monetary policy. The consequences of this new currency policy became readily apparent in the general rise in prices. An index

Chapter 2 The Banking Networks: An Overview

of wholesale prices in Shanghai rapidly increased from 90.5 during the deflationary period of year 1935 to 118.8 by December 1936 (Commission 1936, p. 4).

Many governments around the globe pursued more interventionist economic policies because of the Great Depression. China experienced a similar shift not only in monetary policy but also economic issues, though the shift was driven more strongly by its political unification than by a reaction to the global crisis. The concentration of power and nationwide control by the KMT shifted the previously hands – off approach by the central government, which was admittedly in place due to powerlessness rather than strong "laissez – faire" convictions, to more directed and committed interventions in the market.

One example was the industrial promotion and rural rehabilitation program, which led to initiatives such as the Raw Silk Improvement Committee (RSIC), created in Jiangsu province under the aegis of the government's National Economic Council in year 1934. Together with local organizations such as the Silk – Reeling Industry Improvement Committee, it targeted quality improvements[①] of silk products, one of China's leading export goods at the time, and a reorganization of the marketing of relevant products, including cocoons. To address one structural problem, namely the issue of tight credit, the government involved a number of bankers in the committees, most notably Zhang Jia'ao, the principal director of the Bank of China

---

① As a result of a series of stringent regulations, inferior quality domestic breeds were soon completely replaced by Japanese silkworms. Consequently, the percentage of silkworms affected by disease dropped from 6.24% in year 1930 to 0.37% in year 1935

(Okumura 1979). Programs such as the RSIC indicate that the government involved the banks, public and private, in its interventions and the strategic appointment of bankers into multiple positions was one central aspect of that strategy.

2.2.2 Chinese financial environment in the early 20th century

The Chinese modern financial sector emerged during the first quarter of the 20th century. It comprised banking institutions, financial organizations, and other associations, public and private, handling monetary and financial transactions under the laws and regulations of Chinese authorities while operating along the lines and methods of modern Western businesses (Tamagna 1942, p.5).

This gave rise to the "Three Kingdoms" structure of China's financial market (Cheng 2003, p.10), comprised of traditional, native financial institutions, foreign international banks and the new domestic modern banking sectors. Each of the three came to enjoy considerable autonomy in its specific field of operations and no close, sustained coordination developed between them.

The native money market was formed by institutions dating back to the 17th century, focusing on monetary and financial transactions of traditional Chinese businesses and consumers (Nishimura 2005). They originated according to the product of local needs, remained independent of support and supervision from authorities and established local self-regulated guilds which contributed towards maintaining the decentralized state of activities and traditional methods of management and business (Tamagna 1942, p.5). There is no evidence they

Chapter 2　The Banking Networks: An Overview

financed foreign trade directly or engaged in exchange business (Tamagna 1942; Cheng 2003).

The foreign banking sector arrived in China during the second half of the 19th century. Foreign banks located in a few treaty ports with Shanghai developing as the most important financial hub. Based on concessions by the imperial government to major powers these institutions were legally exempt from the jurisdiction and regulations of Chinese authorities and operated under the control of foreign powers. Their main business activities were to provide financing service for international trade and the presence of international companies in China. In Shanghai, foreign – exchange banks also managed the import and export of silver and international currency transactions. Given these legal and economic conditions, these banks remained institutionally distinct from the rest of China's financial system. The sector expanded substantially after year 1891 when China was increasingly pressured to integrate into the world economy. Additionally, no Chinese financial institutions ever developed into relevant competitors for this type of business[1].

During the final years of the empire and the begin of the republican era, the new domestic banks initially had difficulties breaking into business fields that were traditionally dominated by the other two sectors. Consequently, while traditional, native banks financed domestic trade and foreign banks continued to dominate international transactions, the growth of these new banks was driven by financing governments, including new loan issues and direct

---

[1]　An extended description of the sector, and its separation from ther others, is given by Tamagna (1942).

advances to the government (Tamagna 1942, p. 45.). Nevertheless, modern Chinese banks only played a minor role when the KMT took over the central government in year 1927.

The fundamental changes to the economy and progressive introduction of new economic structures after the KMT's rise to power created a much more favorably environment for the modern banking sector. In particular the new modernization policies, which were linked to the nation's political unification, opened new business opportunities. Additionally, external shocks led to a substantial change in the public perception. In the mid 1920s, several prestigious foreign institutions such as the Banque Industrielle de Chine and the Russo – Asiatic Bank failed, destroying the myth of foreign banks' force majeure with their demise. As a consequence, social elites such as former imperial officials and influential merchants became concerned about the safety of their assets and started to transfer their wealth to Chinese banks. According to reports of the "South Three" and "North Four", two important Chinese bank syndicates, the total deposits of these 7 banks expanded from 140 million yuan in year 1924 to 240 million yuan in year 1926 (Zhaojin 2016, P. 166).

2.3 The Modern Chinese Banking Industry During the Nanjing Decade

Formally, the first Chinese modern domestic bank was established in year 1897, more than half a century after a British bank had set up its first branch in China. The number of banks slowly increased until

Chapter 2   The Banking Networks: An Overview

the fall of the Qing Dynasty in year 1911 and then accelerated during the period of the warlords. From year 1912 to year 1927, despite the political turbulence of this time, a total of 266 new banks opened for business, approximately 18 each year. However, almost half as many went out of business during the same period shown in Table 2.1 (Chinese modern bank statistics from year 1896 to year 1937). Although the historical statistics used by *The National Yearbook of Banks* (1937) have sufficient information to illustrate trends, the exact numbers are somewhat uncertain as details for some banks are rather sparse.

The Nanjing decade (year 1927 – year 1937), saw another period of strong growth in the number of banks established, though in contrast to the warlord era the number of bankruptcies remained considerably lower, specifically a total of 124 new modern – style Chinese banks was established and 23 liquidated from year 1928 to year 1937 according to Young (1971, p. 264). Overall, Table 2.1 (Chinese modern bank statistics from year 1896 to year 1937) presents the numerical development of Chinese modern banks from year 1896 to year 1937.

However, not only the number of modern Chinese banks increased, their total paid – up capital rose from C$167[①] million in year 1927 to C$403 million in year 1936. From year 1927 to year 1936, these banks more than doubled their capitals and reserve funds, tripled their loans and total assets, and quadrupled their deposits as reported by the Bank of China in the *The National Yearbook of Banks* (1937 and Cheng, 2003).

---

① C$ = Chinese yuan.

TABLE 2.1　Chinese modern bank statistics from year 1896 to year 1937

year	founded	bankrupt	net change	year	founded	bankrupt	net change
1894	1		1	1921	27	18	9
1902	1	1		1922	27	19	8
1905	1	1		1923	25	20	5
1906	2	2		1924	7	5	2
1907	3		3	1925	9	7	2
1908	4	3	1	1926	7	7	
1909	1	1		1927	2	1	1
1910	1		1	1928	16	5	11
1911	3	2	1	1929	11	3	8
1912	14	10	4	1930	18	6	12
1913	2	1	1	1931	16	6	10
1914	3	1	2	1932	13	4	9
1915	7	5	2	1933	15	3	12
1916	4	3	1	1934	22	4	18
1917	10	9	1	1935	18	15	3
1918	10	6	4	1936	5	7	-2
1919	16	9	7	1937	3	4	-1
1920	16	14	2	unknown	50	24	26
				Total	390	226	164

Source: The department of economic research of China: Ouanguo yinhang nianjian (The national yearbook of banks [1937]), A7 - A8, A24 - A25.

The growth of modern Chinese banks during this decade was unmatched by either traditional institutions or foreign banks and consequently the sector became the dominant player in China's "Three Kingdom" financial structure. As table 2.2 [Capital power in the

Chapter 2 The Banking Networks: An Overview

Chinese financial market (1936)] illustrates, by year 1936 the total assets of modern Chinese banks had far surpassed those of native banks and foreign institutions combined.

TABLE 2.2 Capital power in the Chinese financial market (1936)

Name/Items	Chinese Banks		Foreign Banks		Native Institutions		Total
	Amount	%	Amount	%	Amount	%	
Note	1946.7	87	284.7	13	0.0	0	2231
Deposits	4551.3	79	511.2	9	673.6	12	5736
Capital	402.7	67	113.7	19	84.2	14	600.6
Total	6900.7	81	909.6	11	757.8	9	8568

Note: Unit: C$1000000.
Source: Cheng (2003, P.78).

Although the emerging modern Chinese banks differed from institutions in the other two sectors in its focus of operations, they followed their Capital Western counterparts by differentiating further along other dimensions. Following a contemporary classification from the *Bank Year Book* 1936, the sector was comprised of the following subgroups of banks:

• Central banking group. These were large public banks under the direction and control of the central government[1]. They only took on direct central banking functions as commonly understood with the year 1935 "Fabi reforms". Central banking groups were comprised of the Central Banks of China, the Bank of China, the Bank of Communications and the Farmer Bank of China.

---

[1] These institutions were not consistently fully owned by the government before the 1935 currency reform, but it had always maintained a substantial stake in them.

- Commercial and saving banks. The daily operations of these banks covered commercial and general banking, including savings and investment business. These banks tended to have a wider branch network while having their headquarters in one of the major metropolitan areas. Banks in this category comprised the biggest proportion of modern Chinese banks.
- Province and city banks. These were established by local authorities as a consequence of political decentralization after the fall of Qing empire in year 1911. Their autonomy from the central government varied with the degree of political control of the KMT over local governments. Main functions included, but were not limited to, handling and coordinating monetary transactions at a local level such as tax collection and the issuing of legal tender notes.
- Farmer and industry bank. Financial institutions categorized into this group were banks whose business focused on agricultural and industrial loans. The origins of many banks in this group had a government background, in same cases these had been established by local authorities with the express purpose of supporting the local economy.
- Specialized banks. Although the business spectrum of these banks overlapped with that of commercial and saving banks, they had a special focus on specific fields such as silk, mining, or salt.
- Oversea Chinese bank refer to banks, whose owners were ethnically Chinese, yet bank headquarters were located outside of mainland China, most notably the British colony of Hong Kong. They also functioned as intermediaries between foreign and domestic Chinese banks given their position.

Chapter 2　The Banking Networks: An Overview

Modern Chinese banks not only differed in their business model but also geographic locations. Although some of them had extensive networks of branches, they did show a strong geographic concentration in their center of operations (Tamagna 1942, p121). It becomes visible in the summary statistics about headquarters and corresponding capitalization shown in table 2.3 (Bank headquarters and capitalization distribution statistics in year 1935). Shanghai was by far the most prominent financial center, Tianjin, a major port in proximity to Beijing, was the regional center in Northern China and Chongqing was a counterpart in the south – west. Banks located in other metropolitan areas fall in the "Others" category.

TABLE 2.3　Bank Headquarters and Capitalization Distribution Statistics in year 1935

Bank Type	Bank Headquarters				
	Shanghai	Tianjin	Chongqing	Hongkong	others
Central and chartered banks	3	0	0	0	1
Commercial & Savings Bank	62	5	5	6	33
Province & City Bank	2	1	2	0	22
Farmers & Industry Bank	8	1	0	0	25
Specialized banks	5	3	3	0	4
Oversea – Chinese Bank	0	0	0	4	4
Total numbers:	80	10	10	10	89
Total assets (in million C$):	4264.1 Mil	438.6 Mil	78.3 Mil	228 Mil	1058 Mil
Avg. assets (in C$):	76149984	54830870	11185961	75996639	13924984

Note: All figures are based on authors' calculation and summary.

Shanghai clearly dominated with 80 banks having their operations headquartered there, a number substantially greater than those of the regional centers in Tianjin, Chongqing and Hong Kong. The aggregate assets controlled by Shanghai banks were over 4 billion C$, an amount almost tenfold greater than that held by banks in Tianjin, the most significant financial hub in Northern China. The average bank size in Shanghai was also the biggest with average assets of C$76149984.

The table also demonstrates that the type of bank influenced the level of geographic concentration. Three of four central banking group banks were located in Shanghai, which despite not being the official capital was the dominant economic, commercial and population center. This is also reflected in the locations of Commercial bank headquarters that more than half of which were located in the city. Banks with a more agricultural or specialist focus were also more likely to be located there, but with shares of a third (Specialized banks) to a quarter, (Farmers & Industry banks) the concentration was substantially less strong. However, none of the other major centers had anywhere as strong a concentration in any of these categories. The difference of strength in concentration points towards the importance of agglomeration forces in the banking sector. Banks with a predominantly financial focus were strongly clustered while banks with a specialized industry or agriculture emphasis followed their customers more strongly in terms of geographical location. Similarly, the Province & City banks clearly showed their origins in and links to regional locations as they were spread all over different metropolitan areas, while oversea Chinese banks were primarily clustered in Hong Kong, the major foreign colony in China.

2.4 Links and Networks

Geographic concentration might be a good indicator for the presence of agglomeration forces, but it does not necessarily say much about the level of competition or cooperation between individual institutions within the sector.

If cooperation between firms within a particular industry is driven by institutions outside of the sector, usually banks and financial institutions act as such third party coordinators. An important mechanism is the access to and allocation of capital (Holmes and Ploeckl 2014; Wilson, Buchnea, and Tilba 2017; Rinaldi and Vasta 2005). In the case of financial sectors, however, usually no such external coordinator exist, consequently I focus on the internal relationship structure of the modern Chinese banking sector to understand how it successfully developed and operated in an uncertain environment.

The idea of strong cooperation within the sector was certainly present in the minds of directors and managers at the time. Leaders of the major institutions seemingly believed that only by cooperating would their banks survive the fierce competition and expand further as detailed in He and Xuan (2015). One practical manifestation of this cooperation mindset was the creation of the Shanghai Bankers' Association (SBA), which was established in year 1918 in Shanghai with the intent to promote not only the welfare of its members but also the coordinate their strategic plans. By 1931, the number of member banks had increased to 29 from the original seven (Cheng 2003).

Practically, cooperation between banks, today as in republican China, can take a number of different forms. One strong link is ownership and control. One bank might directly own another or be at least a large enough shareholder to be able to exercise control over it①. Less strong forms of cooperation are commercial ties and joint projects, and banks might cooperate with other institutions in financing a common investment project, in issuing stocks and bonds, or in accepting each other's issued notes. These have in many, though not all, cases more of an ad-hoc character and not the systematic permanence of ownership and control. Besides commercial ties banks can also have more social and informal ties, which include activities on bank-level, for example membership in industry associations such the Shanghai Bankers' Association (Tamagna 1942, p. 175), as well as on individual level between directors or senior managers. The latter includes common background, such as based on a particular location or educational institution, or common social activities such as memberships in clubs and organizations like the Freemasons. Cliques based on location were clearly an important characteristic of Chinese financial institutions (Sheehan 2005). Such informal ties, however, can lead to another, more visible form of linkage that combines firmlevel and individual level ties, namely an interlocking directorate, indicating that the same person has formal roles in two (or more) financial institutions. Roles can vary depending on management and governance structures, but it obviously

---

① A typical example was the KMT gaining control of private banks through bailouts and resulting nationalizations. For more detail see section 2.6.

Chapter 2 The Banking Networks: An Overview

does require the consent of both banks. Such an arrangement is usually referred to as interlocking directorates.

There are a number of possibilities to quantitatively measure the cooperation between banks within a sector, each with a different focus and reflecting different aspects of cooperation and competition. I choose the network of interlocking directorates because it balances direct, formal links such as outright ownership and informal or commercial cooperation ties that reflect that cooperation arose out of different motives, including direct control, profitability, and social ties, all of which are linked to interlocking directorates[①]. In addition, interlocking directorates present practical advantages for an analysis due to the relative simplicity of the measure, its public nature and consequently the comparatively good data availability over the whole sector.

2.4.1 Interlocking directorates

An interlocking directorate exists between two banks if one employee has recognizable executive roles in both institutions. Although it is possible to restrict it purely to company directors, I utilize a more extensive definition and also include besides directors employees[②] who work in senior management and similar operational roles. There is a substantial literature in finance and financial history that defines and investigates interlocking directorates and the connectedness of banks,

---

[①] The literature concerning the relevance of interlocking directorates for the analysis of cooperation and corporate governance see for example Anjos and Fracassi (2015), Parker and Cross (2004), Renneboog and Zhao (2014), and Larcker, So, and Wang (2013).

[②] For simplicity reasons, in the following I will include these also under directors.

for example Larcker, So, and Wang (2013), Fich and Shivdasani (2006), Field, Lowry, and Mkrtchyan (2013) and El - Khatib, Fogel, and Jandik (2015).

As the names of directors and senior management usually became public knowledge, an interlocking directorate had to be based on tacit or explicit permission of both institutions involved. More importantly, it often was based on instigation of at least one of the banks. One common scenario is that if one bank either outright owns or at least holds a substantial equity stake, then it installs some of its own employees in important roles at the other bank. This can be done for monitoring and control purposes as well as for operational and performance motives[①]. Such an interlock is a link between two firms that can be translated into a network structure with the banks representing nodes and the connecting interlock representing edges. Based on this concept, I am able to construct an undirected bank network formed by shared directors[②]. In terms of Social Network Analysis, I take the banks as actors who decide about forming links between them, implying that edges are the resulting outcomes of decisions by actors, the nodes, and do not constitute actors themselves.

The interlocking directorate network illuminates inter - banking relationships, which reflect a number of underlying economic intuitions

---

① This understanding aligns to (Lan 2015, p. 171 - 183).

② An undirected network assumes that edges between two nodes do not have a direction, so there is no distinguishing of origin and destination for any link. This also implies symmetry, so bank A is linked to bank B and vice versa. For formal network construction and description processes, see Jackson, Rogers, and Zenou (2016).

and motivations of corporate behavior. An analysis approach with social network analysis tools is adopted by a growing literature investigating social connection patterns between companies and related implications both from theoretical and empirical aspects (Jackson 2014; Dass et al. 2014; Parker and Cross 2004; Fracassi and Tate 2012). Particularly, existing literature highlights some features that are important aspects in my setting: bankers on the boards of other corporations can provide know – how and better access to financial support (Gao et al. 2012, but interlocking directors act as monitors and adviser, since those directors are experienced and possess professional expertise (Fich and Shivdasani 2006; Field, Lowry, and Mkrtchyan 2013). Overall, Mizruchi (1996) provides an in – depth examination of interlocks over organizations and systematically summarizes both explicit and inadvertent incentives for the formation of inter – firm linkages as collusion, cooptation and monitoring, legitimacy, career advancement for individual directors, and social cohesion. As the various implications of interlocks may carry as to the corporate governance and management, Brayshay, Cleary, and Selwood (2007) suggests that examination of boardroom networks provides an initial basis for studies of how inter – organization connections may have influenced firm activity.

2.4.2 Interlocking Directorates of modern Chinese banks

As indicated above, this study focuses on modern Chinese banks in the period year 1933 to year 1936 that excludes traditional financial institutions as well as foreign banks. While a number of Chinese banks did interact with foreign financial institutions, the two banking sectors did remain clearly separated. The scenario is similar to the clear distinction of these institutions from the traditional financial institutions. Besides, as I showed earlier in table 2.2, modern-style Chinese banks had risen to dominance by the 1930s with collective bank capital surpassing that of foreign and traditional institutions combined. Consequently, I only look at domestic Chinese financial institutions that were patterned on Capital Western banking institutions.

The main data source is *The National Yearbook of Banks*, which was published by the department of economic research of the Bank of China. The annual issues for the years from 1934 to 1937 contain summaries about the whole sector as well as accounting and operational data about individual banks including names and positions of their directors and managers. I construct the dataset of boardroom composition by extracting information from the summary descriptions of the sector as well as the included annual reports of individual banks.

The data set, which includes names, positions, and branch locations, is used to identify interlocking directorates by matching names of listed directors of all included banks. Due to the structure of traditional Chinese names, duplicate names are not a significant concern. Nevertheless I address this by complementing the basic information about individual directors with information on middle name, birthplace, and age from various biographies and other sources[①].

For a very small number of institutions the recorded data is substantially incomplete or inconsistent. I exclude the small, local

---

① The major data source I use in the article is based on (Jiang 2014).

Chapter 2 The Banking Networks: An Overview

institutions that account for only a minuscule proportion of the full dataset. Consequently, my final sample consists of an unbalanced panel of 628 bank – year observations for the four – year period from year 1933 to year 1936[①]. While the coverage is complete for interlocking directorates, some of the operational and other bank characteristics are missing for a small number of observations.

Table 2.4 (Summary statistics of connected directors and banks) presents annual counts of directors and banks involved in interlocking directorates. Despite the unbalanced nature of the panel being responsible for a substantial share of the fluctuations, a consistent picture emerges that a comparatively small number of directors were linking together a major share of the whole domestic Chinese banking sector.

TABLE 2.4 Summary statistics of connected directors and banks

Year	# Director		# Banks		avg. # busy dirs/bank
	connected	unconnected	connected	unconnected	
1933	148	1267	101	41	1.04
1934	199	1429	114	45	1.25
1935	243	1459	108	54	1.5
1936	169	1530	104	58	1.04

Note: This table presents a summary statistic of the connected director and banks of the data. Directors are considered as connected if they affiliate with more than one bank. Column 2 – 3, and 4 – 5 report the number of banks with connected and unconnected director, separately. Avg. # busy dirs/bank refers to the the number of connected directors each bank on average. See text for the detailed data source.

---

① Specifically, the dataset includes board information of 142, 159, 164, and 163 banks from year 1933 to year 1936 respectively.

Furthermore, the average number of directors per bank involved in interlocking directorates is close to two, implying that many banks were linked in different directions rather than just by a single link[①]. This is confirmed by figure 2.1 (Bank network connections and assets cumulative distributions in year 1933), which shows the number of links per bank in year 1933. Although there is a substantial number of banks that are completely unconnected and some with a single link only, the majority of banks formed part of two or more interlocking directorates. Figure 2.1 also shows the corresponding cumulative capitalization/asset distribution for year 1933. Banks without connections of the total assets in the sector, while 75% of total assets in the sector were occupied by their well-connected counterparts.

As table 2.4 indicates the network of interlocking directorate was changing substantially over the four years. Although a certain amount is due to the unbalanced nature of the panel a good number of banks, according to table 2.5 (Summary statistics of bank board composition change rate) about a quarter to a third, changed their board composition during the course of a year. As interlocking directorates are defined by board members, changes in board membership obviously implicate the persistence and stability of the interlocking directorate network. Consequently, the network was clearly not a static, inert structure but was continually adjusted and modified by the involved banks.

---

① This also indicates that interlocking directorates are not just representing ownership and control.

Chapter 2 The Banking Networks: An Overview

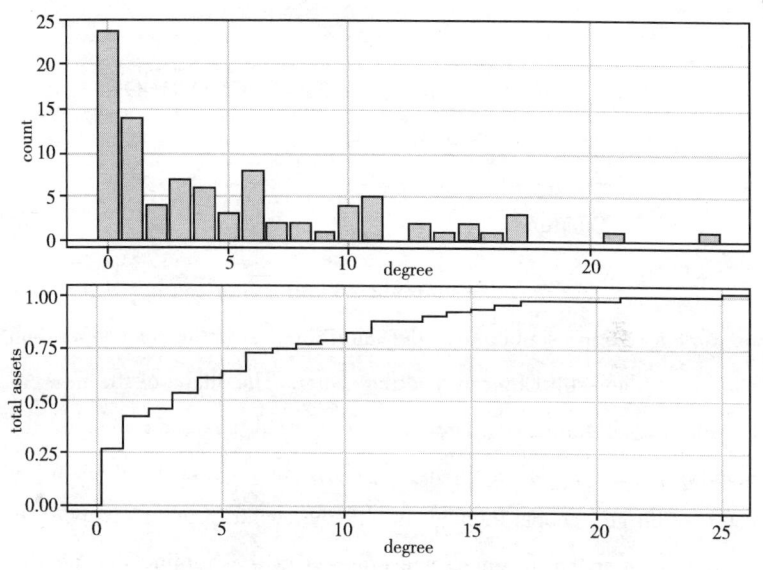

FIGURE 2.1 Bank network connections and assets cumulative distributions in year 1933

Notes: The figure shows a summary statistics of the network connections as well as the bank assets cumulative distributions in year 1933. The upper part of the figure offers the bar plot for the distribution of board connections in year 1933 as example. The lower part of the figure shows bank assets cumulative distributions in the sample for the same year. Details refer to the text content.

TABLE 2.5 Summary statistics of bank board composition change rate

Bank Type	1933	1934	1935	1936
All	base year	0.273	0.293	0.325
Central banking group	base year	0.410	0.155	0.221
Local official banking group	base year	0.256	0.432	0.438
Ordinary banking group	base year	0.272	0.264	0.301

Note: This table provides the change rate of board directors over years with 1933 as the base year. Details refer to the main text.

2.5 Connections and Cooperation

2.5.1 Clusters

The previous section introduced the interlocking directorate network as a representation of the nature and structure of cooperation within the domestic Chinese banking sector. The shape of the network reveals and illuminates a number of internal characteristics of the banking industry. The main aspect I look at here is the question of competition and cooperation. How did the sector structure respond to an environment that despite some progress in the Nanjing decade still was characterized by uncertainty and weak property rights?

Figure 2.2 gives a graphic visualization of the network in each of the four years with the banks categorized into three types, namely the central banking group, provincial and city banks, and regular banks[1].

The four panels, as well as the close-up on a subgraph in figure 2.3 reveal the following about the sector:

- First, the sector was split into one dominant, large principal component with a dense network between the banks in that component and a set of essentially unconnected banks.

- Second, the central banking group banks were all at the core of this principal component as were a number of regular private banks.

---

[1] This groups Commercial & Savings banks, Farmers & Industry banks, Specialized banks, and Oversea-Chinese banks in one category.

Chapter 2 The Banking Networks: An Overview

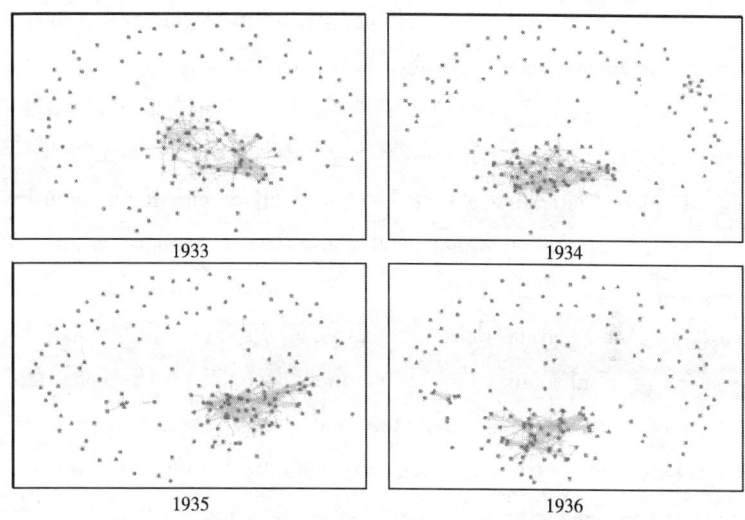

FIGURE 2.2 Bank boardroom network from year 1933 to year 1936

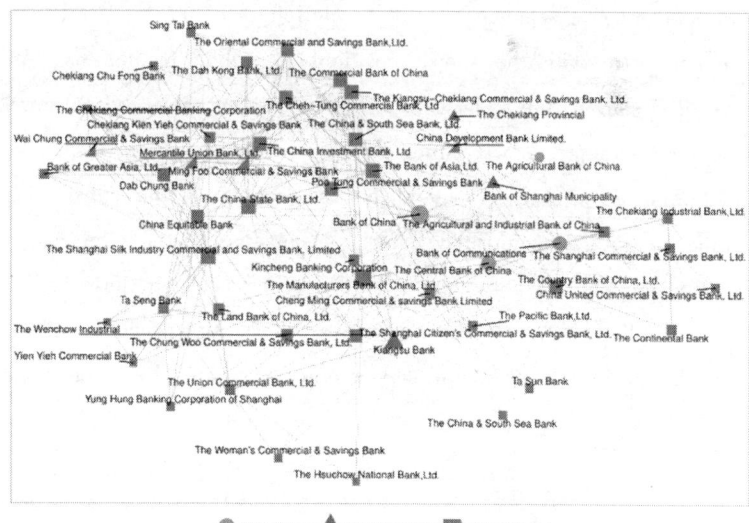

FIGURE 2.3 the principal component of bank network in year 1935

● Third, many, but clearly not all, of the local and provincial banks were unconnected with outside the central component.

These network characteristics lead to some conclusions about the nature of cooperation in the sector. It was clearly dominated by a central cluster indicating a high level of cooperation. If the industry were more competitively oriented, I would expect a number of distinct components, groups of banks, in competition with each other without substantial inter-group links. The absence of smaller clusters and the presence of a substantial number of unconnected banks is consistent with market segmentation where the central component integrates the major economic centers while regional institutions captured a specific local market without strong or even any local competition①.

These two conclusions, cooperation rather than competition and a possible market segmentation at the periphery of the industry, are also consistent with the shown positions of public institutions. As figure 2.3 shows, the major central banking group banks did not form a separate group but were linked widely with private banks. The isolation of local and provincial banks, especially the substantial number of such unconnected banks, in locations outside of major financial centers, is consistent with the hypothesis that these banks were a public reaction to the absence of substantial private banking services and therefore a spatial segmentation of financial markets.

---

① This point is currently more of a conjecture, as the data only displays bank headquarter locations. The existence of branch networks implies that local banking markets could be competitive through the presence of a number of bank branches.

2.5.2 The principal component

The "bird view" impression of the sector shows one dominant network component and a number of isolated banks. This identified principal component of the network represents a large share and core of the sector, as visible in table 2.6 (Summary statistics of bank network characteristics), so its internal structures illuminate the nature of cooperation in the sector even further. Consequently, the following looks at the positions of individual institutions within that central component.

TABLE 2.6   Summary statistics of bank network characteristics

Panel A: Descriptive Statistics bank network				
Year	1933	1934	1935	1936
#Banks	142	159	164	163
#Links	329	458	424	416
#Isolated Banks	41	45	54	58
Network density	0.033	0.036	0.033	0.032
Panel B: Summary statistics of central component				
#Banks	88	89	102	94
Avg. path length	3.026	2.512	3.396	2.903
Diameter	9	8	12	9
Clustering coeff.	0.41	0.40	0.41	0.41

Note: Panel A demonstrates annual summary statistics of aggregate bank Network from 1933 to 1936. A component in network is a subset of the network that all its vertexes are inter-connected. Isolated banks are those nodes, which have no connections to other vertexes in the network. Density is the proportion of observed ties (also called edges, arcs, or relations) in a network to the maximum number of possible ties. Thus, density is a ratio that can range from 0 to 1. The closer to 1 the density is, the more interconnected is the network. Panel B contains statistics summary for the primary component of our bank network. Average path length indicates the average shortest number of steps among two arbitrary banks (nodes). Diameter is an indicator shows the longest number of steps between any two nodes in the network, and clustering coefficient describes an enumeration of the proportion of vertex triples that form triangles, i.e., all three nodes pairs are connected by edges.

Social Network Analysis provides measures about the relative and absolute positions of individual actors within networks (Padgett and Ansell 1993). Here I utilize three of these, namely Degree, Closeness and Betweenness[①].

The simplest measure of centrality is called Degree, which is the number of links a node has with other nodes. Thus, a node a's degree in a network n, denoted as da (n), is defined as

$$degree_a(n) \equiv \sum_{a \neq b} g(a,b) \qquad (2.1)$$

where g(a, b) is an indicator that there is a direct link between node a and b.

This measure illuminates the relative importance of actors, banks, within the network, and can have practical consequences: for example, in terms of information contagion, an actor who is linked with a larger number of other actors is likely to receive external messages differently, potentially more frequently and faster, than actors that are relatively less connected (Jackson, Rogers, and Zenou 2017; Lamberson 2016).

In a network of interlocking directorates, the degree measure shows for each bank with how many other banks shares a director, so has an interlocking directorate. A well-connected bank in this way is expected to have more channels for communications and the exchange of resources.

Table 2.7 (Network and bank characteristics statistics) shows summary statistics regarding the Degree for central component banks.

---

① Literature using these measures to conduct the analysis including Larcker, So, and Wang (2013) and Fracassi (2017) etc..

TABLE 2.7 Network and bank characteristics statistics

Panel A: Firm counts and sample average in the principal component by year

year	Obs.	degree	closeness	betweenness	total assets	estab. year	# staff	# branch cities	board size
1933	88	7.320	0.319	0.025	5.23e07	1924	223	8.7	13.8
1934	89	9.550	0.383	0.019	5.32e07	1924	244	10.2	13.4
1935	102	8.260	0.288	0.026	5.93e07	1924	224	3.7	13.7
1936	94	8.740	0.338	0.022	8.61e07	1924	296	5.4	14.1

Panel B: Descriptive statistics of main bank characteristics in the principal component

	Mean	St. Dev.	Min	P25	Median	P75	Max
degree	8.470	6.570	1	3	7	12	36
closeness	0.330	0.074	0.115	0.286	0.340	0.380	0.518
betweenness	0.023	0.035	0.000	0.001	0.010	0.029	0.267
total assets	6.36e07	1.96e08	9.65e04	3.07e06	7.55e06	3.53e07	1.80e09
est. year	1924	8.3	1897	1919	1928	1931	1936
# staff	247.000	495.000	6	36	61	205	3505
# branch cities	6.770	15.200	1	1	2	6	156
board size	13.700	4.690	2	11	13	15	39

Continued

Panel C: Firm counts and sample average in the principal component by bank type in 1935

bank. type	Obs.	degree	closeness	betweenness	total asset	estab. year	# staff	# branch cities	board size
Central and chartered banks	4	21.50	0.35	0.06	7.68e08	1920	1835.25	14.25	23.75
Commercial and Savings Bank	60	8.93	0.31	0.03	7.68e08	1926	137.04	2.98	13.04
Farmers and Industry Bank	13	6	0.25	0.02	7.68e08	1922	165.67	4.78	16
Oversea – Chinese Bank	3	2.67	0.19	0.03	2.74e07	1920	94	2	14
Province and City Bank	11	5.36	0.24	0.03	4.99e07	1923	228.33	4.17	10.67
Specialized banks	11	6.82	0.27	0.02	1.96e07	1924	79.11	2.11	12.56

The average fluctuates between 7 and 9 over the four years. The high number shows that the involved banks formed a dense web of connections with other institutions. Although there are a number of banks with a single link, the median value of 7 and a lower quartile value of 3 do show that the cooperation in the sector is not just one dominating bank linking to everyone else but a substantial set of connections between banks that are not at the core of this component, indicating the benefit of cooperations were more evenly distributed across the whole sector rather than just accruing to a few dominant institutions.

In addition to direct connections I am also interested in how close each one is to every other bank in the network. This idea leads to the second concept of Closeness centrality. Mathematically, it is defined as the inverse of the sum of all the distances between a node a and all other nodes in the network:

$$closeness_a(n) \equiv \frac{(1)}{\sum_{a \neq b} l(a,b)} \quad (2.2)$$

where $l(a, b)$ is the number of connections in the shortest path between the two nodes a and b. For comparison across graphs and with other centrality measures, this measure is normalized to lie in the interval $[0, 1]$ through multiplication by a factor $(Nv - 1)$, where Nv is the total number of nodes in the network.

The Closeness centrality measure attempts to capture the notion that a node is "central" if it is "close" to many other nodes. In the corporate context, if an actor has comparatively closer ties to more boards, it facilitates better information diffusion and exchange to this node (Larcker, So, and Wang 2013). As more central actors can quickly interact with many other boards across the network these nodes find it easier to profit from the benefits of these connections.

Banks with higher Closeness values are more likely to engage in more exchange of information, which allows them to operate more profitable as well as a better understanding of the outside environment. This easier information access implies an advantage for these banks also in the way they are able to react to changes in an unstable political and economic environment[①].

The results in table 2.7 shows the average normalized closeness values for the four years is 0.288 to 0.383, implying an average path lengths of 2.6 to 3.4 connections. The distribution of the values also show that they are fairly close between the observations with the shortest and the longest average path lengths, implying that pretty much all involved banks were linked well throughout the whole principal component without subsets having been only remotely linked to the rest of the cluster.

Third, I look at the Betweenness centrality measure to understand how central an actor is for the connections between pairs of other actors (Freeman 1977). It highlights the extent to which an actor performs as an intermediary by investigating how frequently that actor is a link in the shortest connection between pairs of actors. A formal definition of betweenness centrality of a node is

$$betweenness(n) \equiv \sum_{j<k} \frac{g_{jk}(n)}{g_{jk}} \qquad (2.3)$$

---

① Recent studies confirm the information spillover of boardroom network as well as other social connections among firms, for example, Helmers, Patnam, and Rau (2017), Hochberg, Ljungqvist, and Lu (2007) and Gao et al. (2012).

letting g_{jk} denotes the geodesic between nodes k and j, where geodesic is the shortest path between two nodes. $g_{jk}(n)$ denotes the total numbers of shortest paths between nodes k and j. Analog of the closeness centrality, the value of betweenness can be restricted to the interval between 0 and 1 through division by a factor of $(N_v-1)(N_v-2)/2$.

A node with a high value of betweenness is prominent, as that actor is in a position to observe or control the flow of information in the network. In other words, the measure illuminates how central an actor is as intermediary between other actors that relies on the importance of shortest paths, assuming that such paths with the lowest amount of steps, and consequently going through the least number of actors, are the relevant connections between two actors in question[①].

In the case of banks as a more central, intermediary position can provide easier access to more information relevant for financial operations. A high difference in this measure also indicates that one bank is substantially more important than another in structuring the sector as it facilitates more coordination between different banks with the potential to improve diversification in geographic or operational focus and to influence others according to its own preferences.

The derived values for this measure as shown in table 2.7 indicate a substantial spread between banks in the principal components. This points towards a core set of banks that did sit at the heart of the cluster without however restricting links between other banks. These more

---

① For a comprehensive summary of the network centrality measure, see Luke (2015).

central banks potentially shaped the internal structure more strongly, however that was predominantly through their influence rather than through direct control①.

Putting the results from the three measures together a more detailed picture of the principal component of the bank network emerges. While there was a core of banks within this cluster, the web of interlocking directorates around that core was fairly strong without clear sub groups or dependency on the core banks. Consequently, the internal structure of this principal component indicates that a major part of the banking sector acted in a unified and coordinated manner rather than outright competition or a separation into linked but distinct groups. Although the sector looked coordinated, this coordination did not rest on the dominant position of a single institution.

2.5.3 Network centrality and bank characteristics

Banks not only differed in their centrality but also in size and related characteristics. Does this differentiation in terms of size not only hold for involvement in the principal component, but also for the importance within the component? In short, were larger banks more connected and more central within the principal component?

Panel A of table 2.8 (Differences in means with alternative

---

① By 1934, the KMT government had direct control over two bank institutions, namely The Central Bank of China and The Farmer Bank of China. But the severe economic recession in the 1930s provided the KMT an opportunity to eventually carry out the so called bank coup in 1935 by private banks been forced to issue new shares to the government, and KMT sending government representative directly on bank boards, hence the core – peripheral pattern of the board network. Details refer to the discussion chapters on silver crisis and economic depression as well as the banking coup of march 1935 of Coble (1986).

Chapter 2 The Banking Networks: An Overview

network centrality measures) clearly confirms that. It shows summary statistics for quartiles based on the number of links. Banks in quartile 4, so those with the highest Degree centrality, were clearly larger in terms of assets, locations, staff and size of their boards than banks in lower quartiles. This result is not very surprising as larger banks were usually more likely to have substantial stakes in or ownership of smaller banks, and interlocking directorates were a related monitoring and control mechanism. Larger banks also operated larger branch networks in substantially more locations, which offered more opportunities for cooperation and led to a higher demand for information from geographically more diverse sources.

Panels B and C of table 2.8 confirm the conclusions about the nature of the principal component. Larger banks not only had a higher degree but also a higher Betweenness value, so they were sitting more central within this network component. This is consistent with the existence of a core group of banks within the network and the domestic Chinese banking sector at large. Closeness however is not substantially correlated with size, which indicates that smaller banks also formed connections directly with each other all throughout the network, therefore reducing the average distances between banks within the periphery of this network component, and consequently their reliance on core banks.

Next to their size and connections, banks in the central component also differed in their business specializations, their headquarter locations and private or public ownership. Table 2.9 (Bank headquarters statistics in the principal component of the network in year 1935) lists statistics about the headquarter locations[①] of the banks in the principal component.

The geographic scope of the principal component shows an even stronger focus on Shanghai than the network at large, which illustrates the dominance of this coastal metropolis for the financial sector in China and the development of a modern banking industry.

TABLE 2.8 Differences in means with alternative network centrality measures

Panel A: Difference in means, based on Degree centrality					
Quartile	size	board size	# cities	sec. asset. ratio	# staff
Quartile 1 (least connected)	15.28	11.92	3.27	0.08	96.75
Quartile 2	15.83	12.28	4.42	0.13	126.10
Quartile 3	16.50	13.31	4.78	0.11	216.10
Quartile 4 (most connected)	17.09 ***	17.89 ***	15.25 ***	0.10 *	582.10 ***

Panel B: Difference in means, based on Closeness centrality					
Quartile	size	board size	# cities	sec. asset. ratio	# staff
Quartile 1 (least connected)	16.04	13.33	9.94	0.10	238.10
Quartile 2	16.56	14.09	5.40	0.12	300.40
Quartile 3	15.78	13.50	3.72	0.12	192.50
Quartile 4 (most connected)	16.23″	14.11 ⁻	8.49 ⁻	0.09 ⁻	260.70 ⁻

---

① In addition to the cities used above I also list Wuhan. Although it was not a treaty port I include it to give a more complete picture of locations, in particular with the Farmer Bank of China, a central banking group bank, located in Wuhan.

Chapter 2 The Banking Networks: An Overview

Continued

Panel C: Difference in means, based on Betweenness centrality

Quartile	size	board size	# cities	sec. asset. ratio	# staff
Quartile 1 (least connected)	15.53	11.92	3.48	0.09	109.00
Quartile 2	16.17	12.51	5.28	0.11	188.40
Quartile 3	15.92	13.74	6.03	0.11	167.70
Quartile 4 (most connected)	16.86 ***	16.62 ***	11.90 **	0.11 *	499.20 ***

Note: The symbols ***, **, and * denote significant difference in means of Quartile 1 and Quartile 4 at the 1%, 5%, and 10% levels, respectively. —indicates there is no statistically differences between observations in Quartile 1 and Quartile 4. Sec. asset. ratio refers to the ratio of sum of bank security to the total assets.

TABLE 2.9 Bank headquarters statistics in the principal component of the network in year 1935

Bank Type	Bank Headquarters				
	Shanghai	Tianjin	Chongqing	Hongkong	Wuhan
Central and chartered banks	3	0	0	0	1
Commercial & Savings Bank	38	3	4	1	1
Province & City Bank	2	2	1	0	1
Farmers & Industry Bank	6	0	0	0	0
Specialized banks	5	2	3	0	0
Oversea – Chinese Bank	0	0	0	2	0

Note: All numbers are based on authors' calculation from the boardroom network in 1935.

The geographic concentration was also closely linked to the different types of banks in the sector. While banks in the central banking group were operating on a national scale as full commercial banks, the provincial banks were predominantly focused on their local home market in providing financial services. Consequently in year 1935, all banks in central bank group were in the principal component and three out of four had their headquarters in Shanghai, while only 7 out of 27 province and city banks were in the principal component, and out of those only two were in Shanghai.

The correlation between spatial concentration and bank type not only held for public banks but also private institutions. Regular commercial banks were overrepresented in the principal component and were stronger concentrated in Shanghai. Only 6 out of 34 Farmer and Industry banks were linked into the principal component network, however all of these were located in Shanghai. This reflects their dual purposes, while some were located close to China's industrial center at the time, the others were spread regionally close to agriculture. Specialized banks were somewhat more geographically diverse as they were linked to different specialized industrial sectors, but they were mostly within the principal component. Their focus on important industries meant that they were either linked to the central banking group banks, reflecting rising government involvement in industrial development or to important commercial and savings banks due to the coordination of private supply of capital to those industries. Overseas Chinese banks obviously differed in their geographic locations as their headquarters were outside the Chinese Republic. With two out of four banks located in Hong Kong, both of which where part of the principal component network, the British colony represented the main gateway for the domestic Chinese banking sector to interact with overseas Chinese financial institutions.

2.5.4 Entrants, Competition and Cooperation

The picture drawn in the previous section indicates that the domestic Chinese banking sector was characterized by a core structure of cooperation that covering all major financial centers and to some degree banking specializations. Although the network of interlocking directorates did show significant turnover, this structure remained consist over the years in question.

In such a system competition could arise either through a group of banks splitting off from the central cluster and creating their own cooperation network or through new entrants that remain independent of the core cluster. The characteristics of the core network structure does not show any indication of such a drive towards a breakup, and even more strongly the low closeness scores also indicate that a large number links would have to be severed for such a breakup.

The Nanjing decade saw a substantial number of new banks created. Given the shape of the network, isolated banks and a central core network could either increase competition or be part of the cooperation within the sector. If new entrants were predominantly isolated, lack of interlocking directorates with existing banks would point towards new entrants fostering competition. However, if they started already as part of the core cluster with interlocking directorates with existing banks, new entrants were supporting the existing cooperation structure and the rise in bank numbers points towards an expansion of the cluster in terms of geographic and operational diversification of the dominating core banks.

To understand which of the two motives, competition or cooperation, characterized the expansion, I look at the average degree of banks sorted into quartiles according to their age. Table 2.10 (Bank age and corresponding linkages statistics) shows the results for each of the four years, including the average age[①] of the banks in each quartile, their network degree and the total number of banks in each quartile. As is clearly visible for each year, newly created banks actually had a large number of interlocking directorates as many as any of the other quartiles. The number of shared directors of young banks (Quartile 4) on average was not statistically different comparing to their oldest counterpart through year 1933 to year 1934. Although the mean of degree (number of shared directors) was significant smaller in year 1935, the value remained still at a high level—on average, the degree of youngest banks is more than 8.

TABLE 2.10　　Bank age and corresponding linkages statistics

Panel A: 1933

Quartile	# bank	mean of bank ages	mean of degree
Quartile 1 (oldest)	18	20.94	10.11
Quartile 2	24	3.95	7.57
Quartile 3	21	11.79	3.96
Quartile 4 (newest)	25	0.60 ***	8.32 ⁻

---

① Banks with missing age are primarily small, rural banks. These did not represent an increased competition as they only operated in their local home markets without competing substantially against principal component banks.

Chapter 2 The Banking Networks: An Overview

Continued

Panel B: 1934

Quartile	# bank	mean of bank ages	mean of degree
Quartile 1 (oldest)	17	22.06	12.65
Quartile 2	16	4.88	9.62
Quartile 3	16	12.56	4.88
Quartile 4 (newest)	19	1.32 ***	11.26 —
age not given	21		

Panel C: 1935

Quartile	# bank	mean of bank ages	mean of degree
Quartile 1 (oldest)	16	23	11.06
Quartile 2	19	5.94	8.12
Quartile 3	16	13.32	4.26
Quartile 4 (newest)	22	2.18 ***	10.82 —
age not given	29		

Panel D: 1936

Quartile	# bank	mean of bank ages	mean of degree
Quartile 1 (oldest)	14	25	13.64
Quartile 2	18	6.61	11.33
Quartile 3	18	14.72	5.39
Quartile 4 (newest)	17	2.71 ***	8.35 *
age not given	27		

Note: The symbols ***, and * denote significant difference in means of Quartile 1 and Quartile 4 at the 1%, 5%, and 10% levels, respectively. —indicates there is no statistically differences between observations in Quartile 1 and Quartile 4.

The high number of interlocking directorates of young banks clearly demonstrates that new banks were built on the expertise, knowledge and support from existing banks. That many directors of the new banks remained active with their existing employers clearly points towards the entry of new banks as an expansion move of existing banks rather than the emergence of new competitors or the breakaway of directors from existing core group of the sector.

That new entry being dominated by expansionary motives is also borne out in anecdotal evidence. For example, in year 1935, the Chekiang Commercial Banking Corporation (CCBC) had been established by Runquan Jin, a financial veteran, who rose to prominence in the Bank of China after starting his career in year 1909 as a branch manager of the Imperial Bank of Qing, its predecessor (XU, GU, and JIANG 1997). Jin took on over time a number of director and supervisor positions with several leading commercial banks in the Yangzi-delta region. Using his social connections and reputation in the sector, CCBC soon attracted a number of promising investors. The board committee included Zuoting Yu, the principal director of Wai Chung Commercial & Saving bank and executive director of dozens of commercial banks in Shanghai. The participation of such "big linkers" granted an advantage of CCBC in gaining internal information and cooperation with other banks. For example, the total asset of CCBC increased from 2091165 Yuan in year 1935 to 2311154 Yuan in year 1936, a 10% expansion in its first year of operations[①].

---

① Performance data extracts from Bank Year Book 1936 and 1937, page D185 and D110, respectively.

2.6 Government and Banking Cooperation

The presence of the central banking group and provincial and city banks clearly showed an involvement of government in the sector. More general, government has a choice between multiple options of how to systematically intervene in the banking sector, most notably pure regulation, full nationalization and individual bank ownership and cooperation.

After the fall of the Qing Dynasty in year 1911, various national governments either had only a limited geographical reach, so were national in name only, or not powerful and stable enough to exert sustained control over the financial industry including the rising domestic bank sector. The political instability explains why no central government was able to achieve dominance over the modern banking sector until the political unification in year 1928 under the KMT government despite a series of attempts by various interim regimes. The lack of power and limited geographical reach also explain why only regulation as well as nationalization were not viable options.

Consequently, I argue that the Nationalist KMT government used the partial ownership of the central bank group to gain influence and even control over the modern financial sector. Direct control over individual institutions, however, only allows the government to influence the whole sector if these public banks have substantial links, formal and/or informal, with private institutions. Influence through interlocking directorates corresponds to the prevailing view among historians that the Nationalists were considerably more successful than earlier regimes in gaining control over and enforcing their will on members of the social elite (Eastman et al. 1991; Fewsmith 1985). Leading bankers, including those that held interlocking directorates were important members of the social elite at the time (Lan 2015, p. 172).

The growth in influence of the government over financial institutions is obvious in the fate of monetary reforms attempts. For instance, in year 1916, the Beijing government had attempted to suspend the convertibility of the currency. The atlempt led to fierce condemnation from bankers and local elites and to a declaration of independence by the Bank of China, ultimately resulting in the government abandoning the policy (Cheng 2003, p. 55). In year 1935, by contrast, the national government conducted successfully a currency reform by introducing a legal note, Fobi, which included the suspension of convertibility per se. This was met with little protest and even with support and promises of cooperation from the domestic banking sector (Young 1971, p. 216). Although the sector was substantially smaller in year 1916 than year 1935, the lower government involvement meant that it wasn't strong enough to overcome the banks' resistance, while the government's hold over the central public banking group and that groups influence in year 1935 was important enough to convince and bring along the rest of the sector.

Chapter 2   The Banking Networks: An Overview

2.6.1   Government involvement with the central/state bank group

The core[1] of the national governments influence were above listed four banks in the central banking group. These were tasked with a number of public functions, including issue of legal tender notes, control over the foreign exchange and domestic money market, and handling of the treasure's funds, with each taking on specific duties (Tamagna 1942, p. 121). For instance, from year 1935 the Central Bank of China acted as the depository and fiscal agency of the treasury, while the Bank of China was the lead bank to handle international exchange. Besides these, the banks were also operating as regular commercial and savings banks in competition with private institutions[2].

Public ownership, or at least a substantial equity stake, meant that the government exercised substantial influence or outright control over the appointment of directors of the central banking group. For example, it appointed the completed board of the Central Bank of China (Tamagna 1942, p. 122). The Bank of China was jointly controlled by the Ministry of Finance and the general meetings of shareholders. The Ministry of Finance was entitled to appointed the bank chairman, 9 out of 30 directors and 3 out of 10 supervisors (Tamagna 1942, p. 127). The government's ability to appoint

---

[1]   Although province and city banks had flourished until 1935, their dependence upon the Ministry of Finance at national level varied with the degree of political control the national government exercised over local authorities.

[2]   This is a summary of authors based on Tamagna (1942, p. 122 – 130).

directors implies that the interlocking directorates between central banking group banks themselves as well as with private institutions were strategic choices by the government. The power allowed them to systematically place the central banking group banks at the core of the internal network of the modern banking sector in China. The KMT thereby successfully increased the reach and strength of its influence on domestic financial institutions and the wider economy through capturing the elites' interests rather than through regulation.

2.6.2 Connections with private financial institutions

This reach is evident in the boardroom connection statistics for year 1935 in table 2.11 (Network linkages statistics between bank groups in year 1935). The central banking group banks, which were fully linked with each other, had 74 interlocking directorates with private institutions.

TABLE 2.11 Network linkages statistics between bank groups in year 1935

bank type	# links	Central	CS	FI	OC	PC	SB
Central	86	0.14	0.48	0.14	0.01	0.15	0.08
CS	539	0.08	0.71	0.07	0.01	0.05	0.09
FI	79	0.15	0.51	0.13	0.03	0.08	0.11
OC	8	0.12	0.38	0.25	0.25	—	—
PC	61	0.21	0.41	0.10	—	0.20	0.08
SB	75	0.09	0.64	0.12	—	0.07	0.08

These links reflect a motivation to spread the KMT government's

Chapter 2 The Banking Networks: An Overview

influence over the industry to control and coordinate the modern financial sector in an uncertain environment, directly or indirectly, even when its official decrees and regulations were hard to enforce.

This is consist with the theoretical idea suggested by Mizruchi (1996), who argues that cooptation and monitoring are explicit reasons for the formation of interlocks and consequently the absorption of potential disruptive elements into the organization's decision - making structure. Inter - banking social connections can reflect therefore attempts by organizations to coopt and neutralize sources of environmental uncertainty.

Boardroom influence was also reflected in the government's willingness to intervenefor individual institutions. In year 1935 a number of private banks ran into financial trouble,[①] while three principal commercial banks, namely Manufactures Bank of China, National Industrial Bank of China, and Commercial Bank of China, obtained advances of C$5 million each from the national government[②] were a number of other banks left to their own resulting in their bankruptcies. As table 2.12 (Banks with central bank connections vs. banks without ones) shows, the three saved banks had existing interlocking directorates with central banking group banks in the years preceding year 1935 while the failed ones did not.

[①] According to The National Yearbook of Banks 1936, there were 15 modern banks went bankrupt in 1935, several others ran into economic distress due to the external shock of the global depression.

[②] The government then converted these advances into equity and nationalized these banks in 1937.

TABLE 2.12   Banks with central bank connections vs. banks without ones

Bank	IDs total		IDs with central bank clique	
	1933	1934	1933	1934
Panel A: Nationalized bank in 1935:				
Manufactures Bank of China	25	26	6	6
National Industrial Bank of China	11	7	1	2
Commercial Bank of China	17	19	0	2
Panel B: Banks went bankrupt in 1935:				
Dan Hoo Commercial & Savings Bank	12	7	0	1
The Bank of Lungyu, Ltd.	0	3	0	0
The Bank of Kiangnan Shanghai.	4	0	0	0
The World Commercial & Savings Bank Ltd	2	2	0	0
Hwa Yih Bank, Ltd.	6	2	1	0
The Amoy Commercial Bank, Ltd.	2	0	0	0

Source: see text.

Particularly, both National Industrial Bank of China and Dan Hoo Commercial & Savings Bank were prestige institutions in Shanghai before the crisis with similar assets, board sizes and business model. However, the National Industrial Bank of China had been keeping a close relationship at board level with the central bank group, as shown in panel A of table 2.12, whereas Dan Hoo Commercial & Savings Bank, with a similar magnitude of interlocks, had only a marginal connection to the state-owned banks. As proposed by the cooptation and monitoring model of Mizruchi (1996), interlocks were used as instruments of corporate control in an uncertain

Chapter 2 The Banking Networks: An Overview

environment and utilized as monitor over the connected firms, influencing the responses of the government.

The above indicates that interlocks of the central bank group provided an extra conduit beyond conventional methods for the government to get operational information of those linked banks, thus shaping the government's decision to intervene and ultimately nationalize only banks with pre-existing interlocking directorates. The contrast in government actions reinforces the impression that interlocks between Chinese banks were an influential mechanism of inter-banking cooperation and control.

2.7 Conclusion

Most studies focus on the impact of interlocking directorates on individual firms, but looking at the network of such links within a whole sector can illuminate its inner workings. The modern Chinese banking sector rose to prominence during the inter-war years, facing a volatile external environment with weak institutions. As their network of interlocking directorate shows, the banks reacted with a strong level of cooperation resulting in a single large cluster.

The cooperation within the sector covered all relevant financial centers and connected banks following similar business models as well as those with a different specialization. Although larger banks were more at the core of the cluster, connections of more peripheral banks were not just to the core but created a close web throughout the periphery. The large number of links of new entrants and young banks also demonstrate that the expansion of the sector in number of banks was driven by existing banks expanding their reach rather than by the entry of new distinct competitors. The network showed a substantial level of changes over years, the fundamental characteristics of the whole sector network, however, remained quite consistent. Nevertheless, the dynamics of the network – formation offers exciting opportunities for further investigations.

The network offers even further insights by reflecting important aspects of the relationship between the sector and government. The central government controlled a core group of larger banks, and through the strong set of links of these banks it was able to exert influence on the whole sector. Direct intervention in an industry through ownership of a few key firms is one particular strategy for government to engage with that sector. The interlocking directorate network of Chinese banks demonstrates the rising central government used this strategy to increase its influence and intervention over an important sector at the core of the larger economy in an environment with weak contract and rules enforcement.

Corporate Policies Propagation Through Board Connection

I employ a sample of modern Chinese banks in the 1930s to investigate how board connections in an inter - bank network affect their corporate policy decisions. I construct bank networks based on interlocking directorates for the period year 1933 to year 1936, and find evidence that corporate decisions of banks are influenced by their social peers, specifically, the more directors two banks share with each other, the more similar are their corporate strategies. The analysis also reveals that peer behavior affects a bank's own decisions not only at the bilateral level but network - wide. Banks with a central position in the boardroom network make corporate decisions less distinctively. Furthermore, the empirical outcomes show that co - moved corporate policies are mainly driven by banks' intentions to pursue profits and eliminate risks, known as profitability and insurance effects. Overall, the findings support the view that banks cooperate intimately with each other at board level and interlocking directorates were a critical channel for sharing managerial practices in the 1930s.

3.1 Introduction

Most researches on corporate financial policy assume that capital structure decisions are made independently[①], in other words, corporate decision making is typically assumed to be determined only as a function of its economic environment, incentive structure, marginal tax rates, etc, but not by direct decisions of other firms. Yet in recent years, a growing literature lays stress on social interactions influencing firms' economic behavior and outcome[②]. Here I demonstrate that links between banks indeed affect their decision making.

---

① Current studies on capital structure decision making generally assume that the decisions are made at individual firm level without considering the inter-firms' impact. For example, Myers (2001), Robb and Robinson (2014), and Hackbarth (2008).

② Examples include studies on the impact of firms from same SIC industry on its corporate financial policies (Leary and Roberts 2014); how social connections in elite networks affect allocation of resources (Haselmann, Schoenherr, and Vig 2018); whether directors and managers belonging to Freemasonry have impact on the performance of companies (Braggion 2011); and how director interlocks, as a channel of resource exchange, produce spillover effects of reputational penalties in cases of financial reporting fraud (Kang 2008).

Chapter 3 Corporate Policies Propagation Through Board Connection

Next to endogeneity and reverse causality, there are three further challenges to identify the effect of inter – firm connections. First, inter – firm links are hard to capture. Current researches suffer from a lack of the unified standard to identify the social connections among firms. Consequently, ambiguous or even contradictory results often stem from various definitions of inter – firm connections[①]. Second, despite the presence of multinational corporations and businesses, most researches on inter – firm connections are restricted to domestic markets of specific countries. Ignoring cross – border connections runs the risk of misidentification in the empirical analysis. Third, sociologists as early as Granovetter (1977) have noticed that even weak ties can be of particular importance in passing information through a network, including labor markets (Topa 2011), criminal behaviors (Patacchini and Zenou 2008), and migration decisions (Giulietti, Wahba, and Zenou 2018). In contrast, most research on the behavioral consequences of inter – firm relations uses a single type of link and has coded connections as binary quantities, either

---

[①] Contemporary studies commonly weave the firms' web by utilizing informal links such as social, educational, or professional ties among executives and directors. But different proxies for inter – firm relations appear to lead to different results. For example, using employment history of CEOs and directors, Faleye, Kovacs, and Venkateswaran (2014) reports CEO connections facilitate investment in corporate innovations, and Dass et al. (2014) highlights that directors with more links to related industries have a positively impact on firms' performance. Contrary to the research, Kuang and Lee (2017) suggests that directors' personal networks have a "dark side", reducing the likelihood of fraud detection, which is harmful to the economic performance. Fich and Shivdasani (2006) confirms the outcome by showing that firms with busy directors (directors that serve on multiple boards) have lower market – to – book ratios, weaker profitability, and lower sensitivity of Chief Executive Officer (CEO) turnover to firm performance.

present or absent.

This paper highlights the issues by investigating the effects and implications of the interbank network in the 1930s China. Besides enriching our understanding of the historical, institutional development of the financial sector in China, I believe that the context provides a limpid environment for analyzing firm – level connections where the confounding effects of the aforementioned challenges are minimized. The underlying reasons are as follows. First of all, the Chinese inter – bank linkages based on director sharing have the advantage of easy and full tractability in a way where the connections serve the need of a universal indicator for network embeddedness. This is because the board level connections depended highly on personal relations (as called Guanxi), which arise from exogenous factors, i. e. "common shared attributes" including kinship, coworkers, classmates, sworn brotherhood, surname, and teacher – students relations (Sheehan 2005). Interlocking directorates, as tractable formal relations among banks, are bound to be adequate, universal indicators for inter – bank relations, which, in turn, reflect the complex personal relations among bankers. This idea is not bizarre and supported by literature, e. g. Granovetter (1985) and Mizruchi (1996), as they claim that interlocks can be used as proxies of network embeddedness. Second, the Chinese financial sector was split into traditional financial institutions, modern domestic banks and international banks during the republican era (Cheng 2003). Each of these enjoyed autonomy in its special field of operations, and no close coordination

Chapter 3 Corporate Policies Propagation Through Board Connection

developed between them (Tamagna 1942, p. 5)[①]. The separation provides an ideal environment in which to test for the effects of business relations among banks without missing international and other outside links. Lastly, the resources of Chinese banks were heavily concentrated in a few major metropolises where banks and bankers could maintain close relations (Tamagna 1942, p. 121). This proximity led to clearer social patterns of relationships[②], which were well reflected in interlocking directorates and therefore easily captured by a single indicator, which validates the use of homogeneous links as is common in this body of literature.

In this paper, I provide systematic empirical evidence about the effect of inter-bank connections on banks' corporate decision making. To track inter-bank ties I use one important network in finance—the interlocking directorate network between banks formed

---

① The traditional Chinese financial institutions had developed in decentralized units without national coordination. Their business was the result of local needs, such as handling deposits, lending, remittances and the exchange of money. Foreign banks were institutions and organizations which handled monetary and financial business under foreign, colonial control. Their activities were directed towards the financing of foreign trade and foreign investment in China. Chinese modern banks in this paper refer to financial organizations and associations handling monetary transactions along the lines of modern Western business methods but under the laws and regulations of the Chinese authorities. Refer to Section 3.2 for a detail description of the background.

② Different types of relationships are mentioned above, but Sheehan (2005) shows that all of them get reflected in identical interlocking directorates. A good literature review, discussing network link strength and homogeneous connections, is Jackson, Rogers, and Zenou (2017).

by shared board directors①. Using a sector – wide dataset of 209 Chinese public and private institutions, I am able to establish annual interlocking directorate networks between year 1933 and year 1936. I use the data to evaluate the impact of social connections on various measures of corporate decisions in three categories: bond – related, cash – related, and reserve – related policies. With a two – stage econometric model, which helps to measure the influence of social neighboring banks on a firm's corporate policy, I find that bank managers were significantly influenced by their social peers when making corporate decisions. Since banks do not choose directors at random, I also explore alternative interpretations and include a number of robust tests to address potential endogeneity concerns.

A social network such as the Chinese banks could be an effective tool to diffuse word – of – mouth information in an environment, where directors and managers faced making corporate decisions without full information about benefits and costs of possible choices. Directors might therefore rely on informal information sources, such as word – of – mouth knowledge to make corporate decisions. Under such circumstances, firms' decision making is de facto influenced by their social peers via interlocks. Here I test if such channels had indeed such an impact on banks' corporate decision making.

The annual inter – bank networks from year 1933 to year 1936, which are used in the empirical analysis, are based on the board

---

① A growing literature in finance utilizes interlocking directors as proxy to study the inter – firm relations and their implications. For example, Kang (2008) and Chiu, Teoh, and Tian (2013).

Chapter 3 Corporate Policies Propagation Through Board Connection

compositions of 209 Chinese banks involving 3 060 individuals collected from the Bank Annual (year 1934 to year 1937), an official record of annual financial statistics, which is also the main source for the bank accounting data used. I introduce a two-stage model to identify whether corporate decisions were affected by peer banks. I use seven corporate indicators as outcome policy measures, which are categorized into three groups. The first contains bond-related policies, since the development of local banking sectors relied heavily on government financing and speculation in government bonds[①]. The second and third include measures for bank risks. I use both cash and reserve related measures to capture banks' corporate behavior from the perspective of liquidity risk.

In the first stage of the empirical estimation, I regress corporate policies of individual banks on common controls, supported by existing literature, to determine the unexplained policy part (excess) shown in the residual for each bank. For the second stage I create an indicator called policy dissimilarity for each possible pair of banks, which captures the similarity in excess policy between the two banks. The measure is then linked to the extent to which the two firms are connected via interlock directorates. The empirical results show indeed that banks linked by shared directors made more similar policy decisions. Furthermore, the extent to which bank pairs are linked, as measured by the number of common directors, is positively related to the extent of policy similarity.

Studies of social networks and their implications suffer problems

---

[①] Refer to Section 3.3.2 for details

of endogeneity. Sharing directors with other banks could be correlated with unobservable manager or bank characteristics that have a direct impact on banks' corporate decision making. This endogeneity issue with social networks is a major concern for all empirical work in this body of literature, and this paper is no exception. However, as the literature has not solved this problem yet, I address this concern with various robust tests and extensions ruling out alternative interpretations of my findings. To rule out the possibility that empirical results are driven by the homogeneity of banks (that is a director tends to sit on boards with analogous characteristics, so that the outcome is only the reflection of the similarity between bank pairs), I examine the attributes of all possible bank pairs linked by interlocks. The outcome exhibits a heterogeneous linking pattern: individual banks tend to link with divergent counterparts differing in major characteristics. I also control for regional effects by selecting the bank pairs only from different regions, which potentially faced different political and economic environments. Again, the results are persistent indicating it is highly unlikely that my results are affected by homogeneity of bank pairs.

Another plausible alternative causal explanation of the policy co-movement between linked banks is corporate control. One bank might be able to control another, so the policy similarity of the pair may be a reflection of decisions unilaterally imposed by one on the other. I carry out a series of tests to explore this alternative hypothesis by restricting the sample to bank pairs that consist of young banks only, where corporate control is unlikely. Results still show the policy co-movement between these banks, indicating that direct control was not the main driver.

Up to this point, the analysis has focused on pairs of banks. Yet individual banks were not only linked to another bank, they were embedded in a boardroom network of the whole sector. A plausible consequence is that the bank's global position in the network also influenced its corporate policy. I test for this by introducing another empirical framework and the use of network centrality measures to capture the position in the network. I find strong evidence that banks with more connections have less unique or idiosyncratic cash and reserve fund related policies.

The final part of the analysis investigates incentives and motivations for Chinese banks' choice to be involved in interlocking directorates. I examine the correlation between the economic performance of a bank, measured by ROE and profit per capita, and the corporate policies I use in the prior analysis (i.e. bond – related, cash – related, and reserve – related policies). The outcome shows that there is a positive and significant relationship between the policy measures and banks' economic performance, suggesting that modern Chinese banks coordinated or imitated the bond, cash, and reserve related corporate policies among their peers in order to affect financial performance, which I call the profitability effect. The aligns with recent research of spillover effects of the social network among firms, For instance, Haselmann, Schoenherr, and Vig (2018) and Chiu, Teoh, and Tian (2013). I also test whether being connected results from banks' intentions to seek assurance and eliminate risk. For this purpose, I use a similar two stage model to that used in the main regression to indicate the excess fluctuation of profitability, and compare it for banks with more board connections to those with fewer links. The empirical test highlights that banks with more board connections have less excess fluctuations of profitability than do banks without links. This result suggests that the connectedness of a bank had an impact on the fluctuation of its profitability, which, in turn, indicates that the motivation of a financial institution to establish board connections was influenced by risk concerns.

This paper advances researches in the following areas. First, it contributes to the literature that explores how inter – firm connections influence corporate behavior and firm decisions. Bouwman (2011) finds that firms interlocked with each other share similar governance practices, which is confirmed by studies demonstrating that directors and managers with social connections are influenced by their peers when making corporate decisions Fracassi (2017), determining corporate capital structures and financial policies Leary and Roberts (2014), or designing compensation and acquisition behavior Shue (2013). In contrast I contribute a focus on a particular sector, modern Chinese banks, which presents a much cleaner and clearer case to determine the influence of peer institutions that are also direct competitors and peers in a strategic sense. In the Republican Era, banks had close links and often shared directors with each other, ensuring that the shared directors were actively involved in daily operations. In the empirical analysis I identify policy similarities in a number of strategic policy choices, which provide evidence that the influence was widely pervasive throughout banks' operational decision – making.

My paper further adds to the more specific literature on

Chapter 3 Corporate Policies Propagation Through Board Connection

interlocking directorates. Although existing studies of interlocking directorates and their implications have grown in volume (e. g. Ertimur, Ferri, and Maber 2012; Bouwman 2011; Kuang and Lee 2017), the literature has not yet reached a consensus whether these interlocks are a clear channel for exchanging resources and information among firms[①]. I provide systematic empirical evidence to firmly support that interlocking directorates are a useful channel to propagate managerial practices, which change how firms act in an economically and politically risky environment.

Finally, my research contributes to the financial history of China[②]. There is limited research on the development of modern Chinese banks in the pre-communist era. Ma (2016), in a vanguard work, looks to understand the successful development of the modern Chinese financial sector in Republican China (from year 1911 to year 1937) from an institutional perspective. Sheehan (2005) also adds to the body of literature by highlighting the network of formal and personal relations in the modern domestic banking sector but does not look quantitatively at their impact. Therefore, Sheehan (2005)

[①] For instance, Larcker, So, and Wang (2013) argues that shared directorates between two boards act as channels of information or resource exchange and that better-connected firms end up achieving better economic results. Similar studies look at corporate governance spillover (Bouwman 2011), facilitating investments in corporate innovation (Faleye, Kovacs, and Venkateswaran 2014), and information diffusion (Shropshire 2010). On the other hand, however, the existing literature also highlights several reasons why having a well-connected board may adversely affect firm performance (e. g. Kuang and Lee 2017; Chiu, Teoh, and Tian 2013; Fich and Shivdasani 2006).

[②] Section 3.2 provides background about republican China and banking in the pre-communist era.

calls on successive studies to answer to what extent operations and capital holdings followed the structures of interlocking directorships.

I contribute to an answer by establishing comprehensive inter-banking networks based on shared directors from year 1933 to year 1936, which is the most critical period in the Nanjing-Decade, and use methods derived from social network analysis (SNA) to show the bank coordination and diffusion of corporate decisions through interlocking directorates.

I divide the paper into six parts followed by a conclusion. Section 3.2 provides a brief survey of the historical background and economic record for this era. Section 3.3 and 3.4 describe the data and discuss identification issues as well as econometric methods. Section 3.5 offers robustness tests, while Section 3.6 explores the overall network effects of interlocking directorates on corporate policies. In Section 3.7, I investigate economic motives of policy coordination among banks through inter-firm connections.

3.2 Background

3.2.1 China in the early 20th century

In the wake of a heavy defeat by the Japanese navy in year 1895, the Chinese Qing empire started on a path towards constitutional reform. Efforts were directly modeled on Japan's thorough Meiji reforms. Constitutional reforms covered broad aspects of government affairs including education, with the adoption of a Capital Western-

Chapter 3 Corporate Policies Propagation Through Board Connection

style schooling system and the end of the traditional imperial examination scheme, and the legal system with a new code and judicial system. Importantly, the so - called "New Policies" recognized the central role of the private sector for a market economy and paved the way for the introduction of property rights that contradicted the traditional philosophy about property, which could be summarized as: *Kings have long arms. All the lands and people belong to the emperor*. However, these reform efforts were short - lived and fizzled out with the end of the empire in year 1911[①].

From the fall of the Qing Dynasty in year 1911 onwards, China was caught in a situation of internal strife during the the era of the Beijing or Northern Regime (from year 1911 to year 1928). During this time span, the country was divided among former military cliques of Qing Army and various regional factions. The era was characterized by constant clashes and multiple military conflicts between varying alliances of these groups[②].

Although the Beijing government was nominally considered to be the central government, actual political power was widely dispersed among local regimes and warlords. Consequently, its influence over local affairs was severely limited, including law enforcement and commercial regulations. Meanwhile, treaty ports, such as Shanghai International Settlement, became de facto foreign enclaves, being legally exempt from the jurisdiction and regulations of the Chinese

---

① For a comprehensive interpretation of the late Qing dynasty, see Fairbank (1978) and Fairbank and Liu (1980).

② Bonavia (1995) details the warlords and political cliques during the post - Qing era.

authorities Ma (2016).

In September 1926, the armies of the Chinese Nationalists, the Kuomintang (KMT), marched into the central Yangzi region, opening their "Northern Expedition" that saw them prevail militarily over most opposing forces. By the end of year 1928 the KMT had successfully united China. Although resistance initially remained, in particular it flared up with the Central Plains War of year 1930, the unification marked the beginning of the Nanjing decade (from year 1928 to year 1937). The era came to an end in year 1937. China's political unification under the Nationalist government provided the modern Chinese economy with a more stable environment for its development, resulting in rapid modernization in urban areas during these years. As a result, by the end of the first ten year (from year 1928 to year 1937) of the National Government, the money market had undergone extensive changes. One the one hand, the modern Chinese money market experienced a transformation from the free-banking era to a government dominated market①. On the other hand, foreign banks lost their absolute control over cost-less and cheap resources, becoming a "necessary cooperation" with Chinese financial institutions, though they remained a decisive factor in international finance (Tamagna 1942, pp. 197-198).

---

① It featured a gradually concentrated market through chains of branches, interlocking directorates, public participation, etc (Tamagna 1942, p. 121). For details, refer to Section 3.2.2 and a summary from (Tamagna 1942, p. 198).

3.2.2 Chinese financial environment and modern banks in the early 20th century

The modern Chinese financial sector emerged during the first quarter of the 20th century. It comprised banking institutions, financial organizations, and other associations, public and private, handling monetary and financial transactions under the laws and regulations of Chinese authorities while operating along the lines and methods of modern Western business (Tamagna 1942, p. 5).

This gave rise to the "Three Kingdoms" structure of China's financial market (Cheng 2003, p. 10), comprised of traditional, native financial institutions, foreign international banks and the new domestic modern banking sector. Each of the three came to enjoy considerable autonomy in its specific field of operations and no close, sustained coordination developed between them.

The native money market was formed by institutions dating back to the 17th century, focusing on monetary and financial transactions of traditional Chinese businesses and consumers (Nishimura 2005). They originated as the product of local needs and remained largely independent of support and supervision from authorities, but established local selfregulated guilds that contributed towards maintaining the decentralized state of activities and traditional methods of management and business. There is no evidence that they financed foreign trade directly or engaged in exchange business. The bulk of funds was invested in loans and advances, mostly to business firms (Tamagna 1942, p. 5, p. 70), and seldom to industrial project.

The foreign banking sector arrived in China during the second half of the 19th century. Foreign banks were located in a few treaty ports with Shanghai developing into the most important financial hub. Based on concessions by the imperial government to major powers, these institutions were legally exempt from the jurisdiction and regulations of Chinese authorities and operated under the control of foreign powers. Their main business activities were to provide financing for international trade and the presence of international companies in China. The sector expanded substantially after year 1891 when China was increasingly pressured to integrate into the world economy. Additionally, no Chinese financial institutions ever developed into relevant competitors for this type of business[①].

The rise of the modern banks as the third pillar of China's financial system was especially strong during the Nanjing decade (from year 1927 to year 1937). It saw strong growth in the number of modern banks established, though in contrast to the earlier warlord era the number of bankruptcies remained low, namely a total of 124 new modern-style Chinese banks were established and 23 liquidated from year 1928 to year 1937 according to Young (1971, p. 264)[②]. Overall, Table 3.1 (Chinese modern bank statistics from year 1896 to year 1937) presents the numerical development of Chinese modern banks from year 1896 to year 1937.

[①] An extended description of the sector is given by Tamagna (1942).

[②] The reason of the liquidation mainly resulted from the worldwide recession and stagflation of the global economy particular during year 1933 to year 1937. A summary and brief discussion of the bank liquidation can be found in Economic Research Office (1937, A. 22 – A. 24).

Chapter 3 Corporate Policies Propagation Through Board Connection

TABLE 3.1 Chinese modern bank statistics from year 1896 to year 1937

year	founded	bankrupt	net change	year	founded	bankrupt	net change
1894	1		1	1921	27	18	9
1902	1	1		1922	27	19	8
1905	1	1		1923	25	20	5
1906	2	2		1924	7	5	2
1907	3		3	1925	9	7	2
1908	4	3	1	1926	7	7	
1909	1	1		1927	2	1	1
1910	1		1	1928	16	5	11
1911	3	2	1	1929	11	3	8
1912	14	10	4	1930	18	6	12
1913	2	1	1	1931	16	6	10
1914	3	1	2	1932	13	4	9
1915	7	5	2	1933	15	3	12
1916	4	3	1	1934	22	4	18
1917	10	9	1	1935	18	15	3
1918	10	6	4	1936	5	7	-2
1919	16	9	7	1937	3	4	-1
1920	16	14	2	unknown	50	24	26
				Total	390	226	164

Source: The department of economic research of China: *Ouanguo yinhang nianjian* (The national yearbook of banks [1937]), A7 - A8, A24 - A25.

However, not only the number of modern Chinese banks increased, but also their total paid-up capital rose from C$167[①] million in year 1927 to C$403 million in year 1936. From year 1927 to year 1936, these banks more than doubled their capital and reserve funds, tripled their loans and total assets, and quadrupled their deposits as reported by the Bank of China in the *The National Yearbook of Banks* 1937 and Cheng (2003).

The growth of modern Chinese banks during this decade was unmatched by either traditional institutions or foreign banks and consequently the sector became the dominant player in China's "Three Kingdoms" financial structure. As Table 3.2 [Capital power in the Chinese financial market (1936)] illustrates, by year 1936 the total assets of modern Chinese banks had far surpassed those of native banks and foreign institutions combined, highlighting the central role of these banks for China's nascent economic development.

TABLE 3.2 Capital power in the Chinese financial market (1936)

Name/Items	Chinese Banks		Foreign Banks		Native Institutions		Total
	Amount	%	Amount	%	Amount	%	
Note	1946.7	87	284.7	13	0.0	0	2231
Deposits	4551.3	79	511.2	9	673.6	12	5736
Capital	402.7	67	113.7	19	84.2	14	600.6
Total	6900.7	81	909.6	11	757.8	9	8568

Note: Unit: C$1000000.
Source: Cheng (2003, p.78).

---

① C$ = Chinese yuan.

3.3 Data and Variables

3.3.1 Sample construction and sources

My study focuses on modern Chinese banks, which I take to include modern Chinese financial institutions, organizations and associates, handling monetary transactions under the laws and regulations of the Chinese authorities and along the lines of modern business methods[①]. My study excludes foreign banks and traditional native institutions, however, as indicated above they did not systematically interact with modern Chinese banks.

The data contains 209 Chinese public and private institutions, resulting in 628 firm – years for the period from year 1933 to year 1936. This is not a random sample, but covers the whole sector. Table 3.3 (Bank annual summary statistics) lists the annual sample size in total and by bank types. The total number of banks increased from 142 in year 1933 to 163 three years later. The distribution over bank types was fairly stable during the time period, though the number of farmers and industry banks jumped from 19 to 34, an increase of nearly 80%[②].

[①] As there is no formal definition of modern banks in literature, the definition used here is from Tamagna (1942, p. 121).

[②] Based on my data sample, the increased number of farmers and industry banks was partly a policy – driven result, however, the incremental fraction largely consisted of those which located in rural areas with small capital. Therefore, the increased bank number in this group does not affect the composition and balance of banks in each bank category.

TABLE 3.3 Bank annual summary statistics

year	total obs.	obs.					
		CB	CS	FI	OC	PC	SB
1933	142	3	84	19	4	20	12
1934	159	4	87	28	6	20	14
1935	164	4	84	31	6	25	14
1936	163	4	78	34	7	26	14

Notes: This table shows summary statistics for the annual bank sample in total and by bank type. Based on Economic Research Office (1936, A5 – A15), I classify the modern banks into six types, which are central and chartered banks (CB), commercial and savings (CS), farmers and industry (FI), Oversea – Chinese (OC), province and city (PC), and specialized banks (SB). Refer to the main text for the detailed explanation.

Information about banks is hand – collected from the Bank Annual (from year 1934 to year 1937) published by the Economic Research Office of the Bank of China, an official annual of financial statistics containing bank – specific information, including accounting data, directors and board members. The resulting dataset lists for each director their name, the position she/he held in the respective institution, the city, and the branch of the bank, for which she/he worked. Due to the structure of traditional Chinese names, duplicate names are not really a problem. To be fully sure, however, I complement the individual director information with middle names, birthplace, and age, which are collected from various biographies and sources[①]. Appendix A.3 offers excerpts from my primary sources

---

[①] The main biographical source I use in this study is an online open database named the Modern and Contemporary Persons Integrated Information System. This database contains various biographies of individuals who worked in the banking sector. For detail of the database, see http://mhdb.mh.sinica.edu.tw/mhpeople/index.php.

Chapter 3 Corporate Policies Propagation Through Board Connection

to illustrate how I collected data from various archives.

Utilizing the board data and the full universe of banks, I constructed an undirected and unweighted boardroom network formed by shared directors to track the informal interbank connections at a senior level[①]. Specifically, shared directors are defined as follows:

- Two banks are considered connected if they share at least one director on the board.
- Two banks are considered not linked if they do not share a director on the board.

As an example, Figure 3.1 represents the bank boardroom connections via interlock directorates in year 1935 based on the definition. The node represents the individual financial institutions, and the edge indicates that two banks share board directors with each other.

As shown, the major banks are heavily concentrated in the central area, as the core, while small commercial and rural institutions are surrounded, representing a core – periphery structure. Based on Economic Research Office (1936, A5 – A15), I classify Chinese modern banks into six groups, namely, central and chartered banks, commercial and savings, farmers and industry, Oversea – Chinese, province and city, and specialized banks. The figure also displays the

---

① According to Larcker, So, and Wang (2013), an undirected network is one in which boardrooms are either connected or not. There is no modeling or assumptions imposed on the direction of the flow of information and resources. An unweighted network is one that does not model or take into account the intensity level of connections between firms. Refer to Jackson et al. (2008) for the detail of network specifications.

inter-bank connections with this classification①. The figure helps to convey the architecture of the boardroom network among banks, which I will use extensively in the following sections.

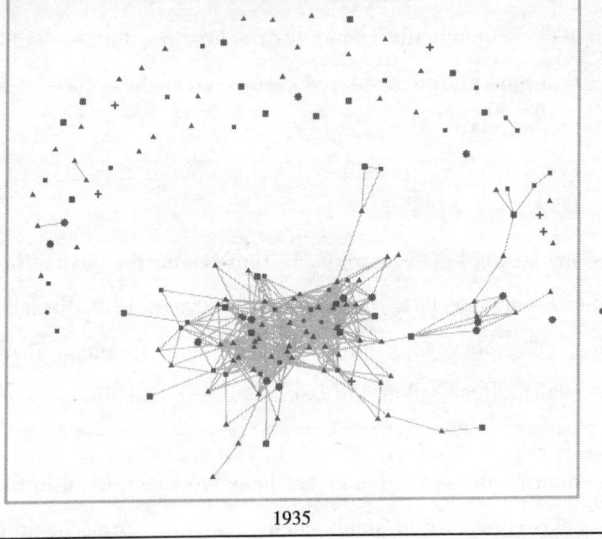

FIGURE 3.1 Bank boardroom network 1935

Notes: The figure represents the network of bank boardroom connections via interlock directorates in 1935 based on the sample. The node represents the individual financial institution, and the edge indicates that two banks share board directors with each other. Different shape of nodes represent bank types. Based on Economic Research Office (1936, A5 - A15), I classify Chinese modern banks into six groups, namely, central and chartered banks, commercial and savings, farmers and industry, Oversea - Chinese, province and city, and specialized banks.

---

① For an comprehensive introduction of the bank classification and the network structure, see Kong and Ploeckl (2018c).

Further, I aggregate the network data, building a symmetric adjacency matrix each from year 1933 to year 1936 at bank - pair level, as it lists which nodes (banks) are linked to each other. The matrix represents the interlocking connections existing among the entire universe of Chinese banks in each sample year. The value in each cell represents the number of shared directors between any two corresponding banks, with the value of zero indicating that the bank pair is not linked. I define the value in each cell as the board link strength (BLS) to capture the extent to which any bank pair link with each other. Taking year 1935 for instance, the dataset includes 164 banks and 1631 directors, I thus have a 164 - by - 164 valued matrix, where the value indicates the BLS. As the adjacency matrix is symmetric, the annual number of bank pairs equals to the number of cells in the upper or lower triangle of the matrix. So the total bank - pair observation is the the number of cells in the upper matrix, which is 13366 $[(164^2 - 164)/2]$.

Table 3.4 [Board link strength (BLS) summary statistics] tabulates the BLS at bank pair level by years. Columns 2 to 4 report the BLS in the sample range with mean and standard deviation, while columns 5 to 8, and columns 9 to 12 tabulate the summary statistics for bank pairs of the same/different bank type with their headquarters in the same/different region, respectively. On average, there is a more than 5% chance that two banks are connected through interlocking directorates. The connecting rate is steady during the sample period, not showing any visible trend (column 3). Banks of the same type are more likely to share directors with each other relative to banks of different types. However, the difference is minor in magnitude (7% versus 5% on average as shown in columns 6 and 8).

TABLE 3.4   Board link strength (BLS) summary statistics

year	total obs.	mean	s. d.	mean—bank type				mean—region			
				obs.	within	obs.	across	obs.	within	obs.	across
1933	10011	0.05	0.31	3922	0.06	6089	0.05	1720	0.24	8291	0.02
1934	12561	0.06	0.36	4421	0.08	8140	0.05	1905	0.31	10656	0.02
1935	13366	0.05	0.34	4363	0.07	9003	0.04	1600	0.31	9131	0.02
1936	13203	0.06	0.35	4007	0.07	9196	0.05	1282	0.37	7763	0.03

Notes: This table shows statistics on the main inter-bank connection variable—board link strength (BLS) at bank-pair level by years for the full sample (2nd to 4th columns), for bank pairs with the same bank type and within the same region (5th to 6th and 9th to 10th columns), for bank pairs not with the same bank type and not in the same region (7th to 8th and 11th to 12th columns). The corresponding sample observations (obs.), mean, and standard deviation (s. d.) are reported. Refer to the main text for detail.

Similarly, banks with headquarters in the same region are bound to have more connections compared to bank pairs located across regions—any two banks as a pair in the same region share an average of 0.3 director compare to just 0.02 of bank pairs with headquarters in different regions. The contrast is driven by the fact that networks after all are geographically bounded: the major banks, which had board links at substantial levels, were concentrated in Shanghai and peripheral areas. In other words, the concentration is less likely to have a considerable impact on my empirical results, since the observations in the subset are relative small (around 1500 within the same region versus around 9000 across regions).

3.3.2 Measures of corporate policy

The richness of the balance sheet data permits a wide range of

Chapter 3 Corporate Policies Propagation Through Board Connection

measures of corporate policy decisions. This study classifies corporate decisions into three categories, namely, bond related, cash related and reserve fund related policies.

The bond – related policies are the main corporate finance measures in the analysis. These results from the generally received view that the expansion of modern Chinese banks during the 1930s was mainly due to their close connections with government, including speculating on government bonds. Modern institutions relied heavily on government financing, and that business became one of their important operations as early as year 1914①. As Wang (1981) points out, Chinese banks charged a significantly higher interest rate by issuing government loans and purchasing government bonds at considerable discounts. Corporate decisions then became crucial for the prosperity and longevity of modern – style financial institutions. Another benefit of having government bonds in the portfolio is that they were not only an investment, but also served as reserves against notes in circulation prior to the currency reform in late year 1935. As a result, government obligations and government – guaranteed bonds constituted the bulk of securities in the vaults of banks Tamagna 1942, p. 136. The bond policy of individual banks reflected the decisions made by principal executives and approved by board members, who could have been influenced by their peers from other banks according to my hypothesis. Consequently, corporate decisions

---

① Existing literature stresses the consensus with ample evidence from different sources. For example, Tamagna (1942, p. 44 – 45), Rawski (1989, p. 137), and Ho and Li (2013).

may include potential impacts from other boards, with which the bank shared directors. Based on this line of thought, I propose three ratios to capture banks' operational decisions on bond holding and purchasing: *bond. deposit*, *bond. loan and bond. SH*.

bond. deposit is the ratio of bond value to the total deposit. It shows the extent to which a bank speculated in the government bond market. Similarly, *bond. loan*, which is the ratio of bond value to the total loan, gives the idea of what proportion did individual bank choose their portfolio to investment into the government bond market comparing to the holding level of total loan. As a complement, I add a third measure into the bond policy group, the *bond. SH*, which presents the fraction of bond value over shareholder's equity. Table 3.5 (Corporate policy measures) shows the summary statistics of the three bond policy measures. I drop a few observations of regional banks due to missing bond purchasing data. The number of bank-year observations ends up being 427. The distribution of bond policy is widely dispersed, ranging from nearly zero to 123% for *bond deposit*. The dispersion implies that policy adoption varied dramatically between these Chinese banks.

The most significant weakness of the Chinese credit system, according to Tamagna (1942, p. 200), was the lack of commercial paper and the nonexistence of a bill market. Chinese institutions were not able to make slow assets in the portfolios liquidatable, despite the attempt by the Shanghai bankers association in year 1932 to establish a joint reserve board. Consequently, banks were extremely careful in coping with the liquidity risk particularly in the banking sector, where confidence and trust was uppermost. Managing their cash holding

Chapter 3   Corporate Policies Propagation Through Board Connection

became an important part of the banks' daily operations in an insecure environment such as China in the 1930s.

TABLE 3.5   Corporate policy measures

Statistic	N	Mean	St. Dev.	Min	Pctl(25)	Pctl(75)	Max
bond – related:							
bond. deposit	427	0.157	0.146	0.0002	0.053	0.215	1.231
bond. loan	427	0.175	0.222	0.0001	0.048	0.229	2.628
bond. SH	427	1.113	1.621	0.0003	0.173	1.399	16.401
cash – related:							
cash. deposit	488	0.134	0.221	0.001	0.034	0.134	2.900
cash. loan	489	0.164	0.567	0.0003	0.029	0.122	8.292
reserve fund – related:							
reserve. loan	437	0.047	0.073	0.0001	0.013	0.055	0.775
reserve. deposit	436	0.071	0.274	0.0001	0.014	0.062	4.700

Notes: This table provides a statistical summary of the corporate policy measures in this article. Policies are classified into three categories, namely bond, cash, and reserve fund related policy. N refers to the number of observations. For details refers to the main text.

As the next set of measures, I therefore introduce policy indicators regarding the banks' liquidity risk. In particular, two measures are used to evaluate these cash related policies, which are *cash deposit* and *cash loan*. The measures are defined as the ratio of cash holding over the aggregate deposit and loan, respectively. As Table 3.5 reports, the cash – related measures are widely distributed from zero to 2.9 for *cash deposit* and 8.3 for *cash loan*.

A concern about these cash related measures is that they may not precisely reflect the liquidity risk as major Chinese banks, not just limited to the central banking group, enjoyed the privilege of note issue before the currency reform in late 1935[①]. As a consequence, they could issue legal tender notes when cash reserve runs low. I thus introduce another measure to gauge bank liquidity risk by calculating reserve fund related indicators. I use *reserve loan* (the ratio of reserve fund of a bank to its total loan) and *reserve deposit* (the ratio of reserve fund of a bank to its total deposit) as a reflection of such managerial decisions. Their definitions are akin to that of cash-related measures, but the numbers vary within a more acceptable range (from 0 to less than five) as the table (last two rows) presents.

3.3.3 Control variables

Estimating the pair model requires two sets of control variables, one set designed to explain the variation within bank pairs, while another one, based on firm characteristics, controls for bank level variation. I detail the variables and provide descriptive statistics in the following table.

3.3.3.1 Bank characteristics

Descriptive statistics on the controls are provided in Table 3.6 (Bank level controls). Firm characteristics are listed under three headings: bank basics, performance, and financial measures. Appendix A.1 describes the definitions of the variables.

[①] At the end of 1934, the right to issue notes was still granted to commercial banks. For detail of note issue and the currency reform in 1935, refer to Section 3.2 and Young (1971, Part Three).

Chapter 3 Corporate Policies Propagation Through Board Connection

TABLE 3.6   Bank level controls

Statistic	N	Mean	St. Dev.	Min	Max
Bank basics:					
est. year	585	1926	7.649	1897	1936
# staff	471	180	393	5	3505
# cities	469	5.5	12	1.000	156
if. connected	628	0.69	0.46	0	1
board size	470	12.8	4.701	1	39
total assets (in millions)	489	41.43	153.13	42.1	1803
Performance measures:					
net profit	468	327636	1275358	15	17095868
RoE	468	0.130	0.373	0.0003	7.950
profit per capita	455	1543.8	1925.9	2.5	19076.3
Operational variables:					
reserve fund	437	748192.300	2023860	30	23903709
deposits all kinds	488	27927641	103351102	4970	1206305176
loans all kinds	489	23062044	85427107	32033	962871078
paid in Capital	489	2682052	8757515	32650	100000000
cash on hand	489	4149788	21474528	137	307865614
total expenditure	483	484004	1303923	1391	11422324
total income	486	789728	2297073	1959	25964686
investment in securities	427	4155334	16021991	28	252904406

Notes: This table lists the bank level characteristics in summary. The calculation is based on the sample cross all years in the dataset. N refers to the number of observations. Variable definitions and descriptions are provided in Appendix A.1.

The set of basic bank variables includes variables describing the main characteristics; *est. year* reports the year in which each bank was founded. The modern bank sector was relatively young, as the first institution was founded in year 1897 and the mean year of establishment is 1926. I also include two variables (# *staff* and # *cities*) to capture the sizes of individual banks. Further, I add two board level controls to capture governance and control characteristics with the number of directors (board size) ranging from 1 to 39. The board connection (if. connected) dummy serves as a proxy to catch potential external influence. It takes the value of 1 if, as defined above, the director of a bank was serving as director in at least one other bank.

Tamagna (1942, p. 121) argues that the resources of modern banks were heavily concentrated and their centers were located in the modern commercial cities. This claim is largely supported by the variables in the basic bank variable set. The variations of staff number (# *staff*), cities in which banks do business (# *cities*), number of board directors (*board size*), and total assets are extremely high. The Bank of China alone had the largest number of staff (3505 employees), board size (39 directors on the board), assets (over CSD $1.8 billion) and its business/branches covered 156 cites in China, while some small and local institutions had retained a family-scale pattern (as shown in the Min column of Table 3.6).

The performance measures are net profit, return on assets (ROA), and return on equity (ROE). Net profit is an absolute gauge of bank performance. The variation of the measure is substantial, ranging from nearly zero to over CSD$ 17 millions.

Chapter 3 Corporate Policies Propagation Through Board Connection

Surprisingly, I do not observe any institution that ended up at a loss during the sample period (the minimum net profit is CSD $15). I confirm the result by cross-checking the existing literature and consulting with historians. The only information available about the issue is from Economic Research Office (1937, A7 - A8, A24 - A25), which shows that 29 modern banks went bankrupt from year 1933 to year 1936. However, the details of the financial status of those bankrupted banks are not available. The second measure of performance (ROE) is profitability measured as returns (*net profit*) over equity. Profits are computed after taxes and interest. Average ROE ranges from 0 to 795%, which presents a disparate profit margin in the sector, again consistent with the resource concentration argument mentioned in the earlier section. Third, in view of worker productivity, I add *profit per capita* as a supplementary performance measure. It indicates the average efficiency per employee as *net profit* over # *staff*. Due to the missing data issue, the number of observation declines slightly to 455 as compared to 468 for both *net profit* and ROE.

Additionally, Table 3.6 provides summary statistics of the operational variables that I will use in the empirical section. These variables are comprised of accounting items extracted from banks' balance sheets. The variables are mainly used to quantify the corporate policy, as detailed in section 3.3.2. All values are in Chinese silver dollars (CSD).

3.3.3.2 Bank pair level controls

One feature of the study is that I propose a two-stage firm pair model to evaluate the influence of board connections on the similarity in banks' corporate policies. To carry out the analysis, I need not only bank characteristics as controls, but also variables at the pair level. Table 3.7 (Bank pair level variables summary) reports summary statistics of the included variables for the model. Panel A highlights the key indicators that I use to measure the policy dissimilarity among bank pairs, while Panel B lists the intra-pair controls used in the regressions. These are variables that combine the characteristics of both banks. The characteristics of the pair of banks include the number of board directors, whether two banks belong to the same type, asset size, ROE total staff number, and the cities in which they set up branches. Appendix A.1 provides the details of the variable definitions. Section 3.4.1 discusses the variables further as part of the introduction of the pair model.

TABLE 3.7 Bank pair level variables summary

Panel A: Policy dissimilarity							
Variable	N	Mean	St. Dev.	Min	Pctl(25)	Pctl(75)	Max
bond related policy measures							
bond. deposit	39238	0.072	0.075	0.000	0.022	0.096	0.702
bond. loan	39238	0.107	0.120	0.000	0.032	0.137	1.146
bond. SH	39238	0.410	0.354	0.000	0.147	0.586	2.483
cash related policy measures							
cash. deposit	47048	0.062	0.084	0.000	0.015	0.075	0.781
cash. loan	47048	0.116	0.240	0.000	0.023	0.106	2.139
reserve fund related policy measures							
reserve. loan	41054	0.025	0.043	0.000	0.005	0.025	0.380
reserve. deposit	41054	0.041	0.110	0.000	0.008	0.040	1.115

Chapter 3 Corporate Policies Propagation Through Board Connection

Continued

Panel B: Bank - pair level controls

agg. dir	47048	25.706	6.651	2	22	29	66
diff. dir	47048	4.918	4.483	0	2	7	38
same. type	47048	0.330	0.470	0	0	1	1
diff. asset	47048	2.243	1.701	0.0001	0.873	3.268	9.977
diff. RoE	47048	0.268	0.572	0.004	0.144	0.283	8.533
agg. staff	47048	384.848	575.565	13	82	405.2	5823
diff. staff	47048	269.902	513.096	0	24	271	3499
agg. dty	47048	11.339	24.798	2	2	10	312
diff. city	47048	7.233	15.778	0	1	7	155

Notes: The table shows a summary statistics of the variables at bank pair level. Two banks are considered as a pair when they linked through interlocking directorates. N refers to the number of observations. Panel A reports the certain policy dissimilarity measures between any two pair, while panel B gives a statistic summary of the pair controls using in the regression.

3.4 The Impact of Inter-bank Ties on Corporate Policy

In this section, I investigate the influence of inter-bank connections on banks' corporate policies. I introduce a model to carry out the quantitative analysis that examines the similarity in various policies between bank pairs, and then report the results.

3.4.1 The empirical framework: Pair model

I propose a pair model to examine the influence of interlocking directorates on banks' operational behavior. The model is inspired by and derived from Fracassi (2017). The analysis is based on each possible pair of banks in the sample as the unit. For instance, given 142 banks from the data set in year 1933 leads to over 10 000 distinct pairs under examination①. For each pair of firms, I measure the strength of their connectedness through interlock directorates according to the number of directors shared by the two banks. This basic model setup is then used to test whether two banks linked though board interlocks have similar or dissimilar operational policy/ corporate decision.

The estimation is comprised of two parts. In the first stage, I account for a bank's corporate policy using common controls. For each bankyear, I obtain a residual, which contains the excessive policy that is not explained by the included control variables. I compare these residuals (or excessive policy) for each pair of banks to derive a indicator of policy dissimilarity. The second stage then examines whether interbank board relations are related to the similarity in policy between the bank pair.

More specifically, I run a regression of individual bank i's operational variables at year t on control variables $X_{i,t}$, as proposed by the existing literature, in the first stage, as shown in equation 3.1:

$$Corporate\ policy_{i,t} = \alpha_0 + \alpha_1 X_{i,t} + FE_i + FE_t + \varepsilon_{i,t} \quad (3.1)$$

---

① I use a symmetric matrix to represent the boardroom connections between any two banks, with each cell indicating the number of shared directors. The number of possible bank pairs in 1933 then equals the number of cells in the upper or lower triangle of the matrix, which is $(142^2 - 142)/2 = 10,011$.

Chapter 3 Corporate Policies Propagation Through Board Connection

As the corporate policy outcome variables, I classify seven measures into bond, cash, and reserve – related groups as discussed in section 3.3.2. As controls, I add year and bank fixed effects to control for bank and time invariant factors. The residual $\varepsilon_{i,t}$ includes the idiosyncratic part of the corresponding corporate decision that have not been captured by the conventional factors, as $X_{i,t}$ in the equation 3.1. Table 3.8 (Pair model: first stage regression) reports the result of the first stage according to equation 3.1. The coefficients of the controls are in line with results from the existing literature.

For each possible pair i and j, I then define corporate policy dissimilarity as the absolute value of the difference in their residuals:

$$\text{Policy dissimilarity} = |\varepsilon_{i,t} - \varepsilon_{j,t}| \qquad (3.2)$$

The measure describes how different are the corporate decisions that have been adopted by the pair of banks. A larger value of this dissimilarity measure indicates more differences in the policies chosen by those two banks, and vice versa. This proxy is used to compare the potential policy deviation among any pair of banks.

The second stage of the model assesses whether and how inter-banking connections influence banks' operational behavior. I regress the log of the policy dissimilarity over the lagged natural logarithm of the interbanking links $BLS_{i,j}$ between bank i and j. $BLS_{i,j}$ is used as a proxy to indicate the link strength of each bank pair. For example, if there is no shared director between bank i and j, then $BLS_{i,j} = 0$. Accordingly $BLS_{i,j} = 3$ denotes that three directors sit on the boards of both banks. Mathematically, I define the model as:

$$\ln(1 + |\Delta\varepsilon_{i,j,t}|) = \beta_0 + \beta_1 \ln(1 + BLS_{i,j,t-1}) + X_{P,i,j,t-1} + \eta_{i,j,t}$$
$$(3.3)$$

TABLE 3.8　　Pair model: first stage regression

	Dependent variable:						
	bond. deposit	bond. loan	bond. SH	cash. deposit	cash. loan	reserve. loan	reserve. deposit
	(1)	(2)	(3)	(4)	(5)	(6)	(7)
ln（assets）	0.043 (0.026)	0.171*** (0.049)	1.436*** (0.268)	0.026 (0.028)	0.187 (0.129)	0.007 (0.012)	0.066 (0.045)
RoE	-0.576*** (0.140)	-1.053*** (0.261)	-1.457 (1.416)	0.102 (0.145)	-0.257 (0.669)	-0.004 (0.062)	-0.078 (0.228)
#cities	-0.00004 (0.001)	0.001 (0.001)	0.011 (0.007)	-0.001 (0.001)	-0.001 (0.004)	0.0003 (0.0003)	0.0003 (0.001)
board size	o.oir* (0.005)	0.012 (0.009)	0.026 (0.049)	-0.002 (0.004)	-0.007 (0.021)	-0.002 (0.002)	-0.002 (0.007)
ln（total expenditure）	-0.016 (0.028)	0.042 (0.052)	0.208 (0.284)	-0.031 (0.031)	0.047 (0.143)	-0.016 (0.015)	0.021 (0.056)
ln（total income）	0.039 (0.034)	-0.003 (0.063)	-0.470 (0.344)	0.051 (0.038)	-0.029 (0.173)	0.045*** (0.017)	0.071 (0.062)
ln（fixed assets） -0.001	0.022 (0.009)	-0.005 (0.017)	-0.008 (0.095)	0.010 (0.010)	0.046 (0.046)	0.004 (0.004)	(0.016)

Continued

	Dependent variable:						
	bond. deposit	bond. loan	bond. SH	cash. deposit	cash. loan	reserve. loan	reserve. deposit
	(1)	(2)	(3)	(4)	(5)	(6)	(7)
if. connected	-0.013	-0.003	0.230	-0.030	-0.021	-0.004	-0.025
	(0.029)	(0.054)	(0.294)	(0.029)	(0.135)	(0.013)	(0.047)
ln(#staff)	-0.056*	-0.092*	-0.225	-0.040	-0.255*	-0.044***	-0.171***
	(0.029)	(0.055)	(0.298)	(0.032)	(0.146)	(0.014)	(0.051)
Constant	-151.381**	-329.141***	-2025.206***	39.892	-30.035	-3.690	-65.627
	(67.266)	(125.415)	(680.798)	(73.662)	(339.099)	(30.802)	(114.253)
Year FE	Yes	Yes	Yes	Yes	Yes	Yes	Yes
Individual FE	Yes	Yes	Yes	Yes	Yes	Yes	Yes
Observations	374	374	374	409	409	382	382
Adjusted R^2	0.563	0.377	0.665	0.748	0.265	0.625	0.659

Notes: $*p<0.1$; $**p<0.05$; $***p<0.01$. This table presents the empirical results of the first stage with different dependent variables, which are shown in the header line.

I take the suggestion of Fracassi (2017), adding $X_{P,i,j,t-1}$ as lagged pair-wise control in the second-stage specification, even though determinants of firm policy are already controlled for in the first stage. A benefit of doing this is that it controls for potential heteroscedasticity that may lead to a biased result. For instance, if banks of a particular type have greater policy dispersion across pairs than other bank types (i.e. heteroskedasticity in the error term), then belonging to that bank type may still influence the similarity in policies across bank pairs. The extra control setting includes the combination of factors over the two banks, covering different aspects of the attributes of the pair. Panel B of Table 3.7 provides a summary statistics of the variables for reference, and the detailed definition of them is given in Appendix A.1.

3.4.2 The main results

Table 3.9 (2nd. stage regression: bond policy dissimilarities) reports the estimation of the relationship between bond policies and inter-bank links via shared directors according to equation 3.3. I use three major policy indicators as dependent variables, namely, bond-deposit ratio, bond-loan ratio, and bond-shareholder equity ratio with each outcome estimation including three columns for various specifications. First, columns (1), (4) and (7) present the baseline regressions that only include link strength with no further controls. Theoretically, the second stage regressions do not need extra controls as profitability, bank and pair characteristics, years are controlled at the first stage. I find a strong and negative impact of inter-bank connections on the bond policy dissimilarities, measured by all those three indicators, which should be considered as firm evidence

Chapter 3 Corporate Policies Propagation Through Board Connection

TABLE 3.9 2nd. stage regression: bond policy dissimilarities

Dependent variable:

	bond. deposit			bond policy dissimilarity bond. loan			bond. SH		
	(1)	(2)	(3)	(4)	(5)	(6)	(7)	(8)	(9)
BLS	-0.018*** (0.002)	-0.016*** (0.002)	-0.013*** (0.002)	-0.024*** (0.004)	-0.027*** (0.004)	-0.028*** (0.004)	-0.037*** (0.011)	-0.014 (0.010)	-0.043*** (0.010)
agg. dir			-0.00004 (0.0001)			0.001*** (0.0002)			-0.004*** (0.0004)
agg. staff			-0.00001*** (0.00000)			-0.00001** (0.00000)			0.0002*** (0.00001)
agg. city			-0.00001 (0.00002)			-0.00002 (0.00004)			0.00004 (0.0001)
diff. asset		0.001** (0.0004)	0.0002 (0.0004)		-0.002*** (0.001)	-0.002*** (0.001)		0.001 (0.002)	0.009*** (0.002)
diff. city		-0.00002 (0.00004)	0.00000 (0.00005)		0.00002 (0.0001)	0.00002 (0.0001)		0.002*** (0.0002)	0.002*** (0.0002)
d iff. staff		-0.00001*** (0.00000)	0.00001*** (0.00000)		-0.00000 (0.00000)	0.00001 (0.00001)		0.00002*** (0.00001)	-0.0002*** (0.00002)

Continued

		bond. deposit			bond policy dissimilarity bond. loan				bond. SH	
Dependent variable:	(1)	(2)	(3)	(4)	(5)	(6)	(7)	(8)	(9)
diff RoE		0.134*** (0.004)	0.135*** (0.004)		0.400*** (0.007)	0.406*** (0.007)		1.220*** (0.018)	1.166*** (0.018)
same. type		−0.016*** (0.001)	−0.016*** (0.001)		−0.018*** (0.002)	−0.019*** (0.002)		−0.011** (0.005)	−0.004 (0.005)
Constant	0.074*** (0.001)			0.115*** (0.001)			0.419*** (0.003)		
Year FE	No	Yes	Yes	No	Yes	Yes	No	Yes	Yes
Pair FE	No	No	Yes	No	No	Yes	No	No	Yes
Observations	22848	22848	22848	22848	22848	22848	22848	22848	22848
Adjusted R^2	0.003	0.056	0.057	0.002	0.148	0.149	0.0005	0.191	0.203

Notes: * $p < 0.1$; ** $p < 0.05$; *** $p < 0.01$. This table presents the empirical results of the second stage with bond related policy dissimilarities as dependent variables. Definitions of the variables are provides in Appendix A.1.

Chapter 3 Corporate Policies Propagation Through Board Connection

supporting the hypothesis that banks use interlocking directorates as a channel to coordinate their operational policies.

In columns (2), (5) and (8) of Table 3.9, I add several control variables across the three diffcrent policies. First, I add the differences in assets, cities covered, staff number, and ROE, between the paired banks to rule out that similarity in bond policy is driven by similarity in bank size and profitability. As Figure 3.1 illustrates, board connections tended to be common among commercial banks, and the "Big Four" in the central bank group were fully linked across the sample years. To consider such heteroskedasticity, I also add a bank type dummy variable that takes the value of 1 if both banks in a pair belong to the same bank type. For the same reason, a year dummy is added in the specifications to control for idiosyncratic difference in the second stage regression across years. The sign of dependent variable bond/SH is negative, but loses its significance. Overall, the empirical result remains unchanged after the controls as the coefficients on BLS stay negative and statistically significant for both bond/deposit and bond/loan ratio.

In columns (3), (6) and (9) of Table 3.9, I add more controls to allow for the fact that larger and more experienced financial institutions tended to have more board connections. The add. dir, agg. staff, and agg. city variables are the number of total directors, staff, branch cities covered respectively for each bank pair. I also consider a pair fixed effect in the regression models. Again, the empirical outcomes confirm the main hypothesis, and are consistent with the results above. In general, I find strong evidence that BLS affected the banks' dissimilarity of bond - related operational policies negatively during my sample period, i. e. a bank pair tended to adopt similar policy if they were connected via interlocking directorates.

Next, I interpret the economic magnitude of the results. Recall that in the second stage of the pair model, as defined in Equation 3.3, both the dependent variable and BLS are in terms of logs. Consequently, the empirical outcomes of (1) to (3) imply that two board - linked banks had bond/deposit ratios that were on average 1.5% more similar than those of an unconnected pair In addition, the economic magnitude is even greater (between 2.5% and 4%) for bond/loan and bond/shareholder equity ratios. These are lower bound estimates of the real effects of board ties on corporate policies, given the noise in the definition of inter - bank connections. The results are robust and persistent across all bond - related dependent variables. So the presence of board connection strikingly reduced policy dissimilarity among linked banks, suggesting modern Chinese banks coordinated their operational decisions with interlocking directorates as an important information exchange channel.

Table 3.10 (2nd. stage regression: cash policy dissimilarities) and table 3.11 (2nd. stage regression: reserve fund policy dissimilarities) show the second stage regressions for cash and reserve fund related policies based on the same empirical strategy. I find that the intensity of ties still predicts similar cash and reserve policies even for firm pairs. Furthermore, the economic magnitudes of the effects of cash and reserve related policies are similar to the estimate for bond policy. Two companies that are connected have cash policies that are 1% to 4% (Table 3.10) or reserve policy that are 1% to 2% (Table 3.11) more similar than for two unconnected firms.

TABLE 3.10 2nd. stage regression: cash policy dissimilarities

	Dependent variable:					
	cash. deposit		cash policy dissimilarity		cash. loan	
	(1)	(2)	(3)	(4)	(5)	(6)
BLS	−0.006** (0.003)	−0.013*** (0.003)	−0.007*** (0.003)	−0.035*** (0.007)	−0.047*** (0.007)	−0.050*** (0.008)
agg. dir			−0.003*** (0.0001)			−0.008*** (0.0003)
agg. staff			0.00004*** (0.00000)			0.0002*** (0.00001)
agg. city			−0.00001 (0.00002)			0.00004 (0.0001)
diff. asset		−0.0004 (0.0004)	0.0003 (0.0004)		−0.002* (0.001)	0.003** (0.001)
diff. city		0.0001 (0.00004)	0.0002*** (0.00005)		0.001*** (0.0001)	0.001*** (0.0001)
diff. staff		0.00001*** (0.00000)	−0.00001*** (0.00000)		0.00001* (0.00001)	−0.0001*** (0.00001)

Continued

	Dependent variable:					
	cash. deposit		cash policy dissimilarity		cash. loan	
	(1)	(2)	(3)	(4)	(5)	(6)
diff. RoE		−0.057*** (0.004)	−0.090*** (0.004)		−0.185*** (0.013)	−0.278*** (0.013)
same. type		−0.022*** (0.001)	−0.021*** (0.001)		−0.063*** (0.003)	−0.056*** (0.003)
Constant	0.065*** (0.001)			0.125*** (0.002)		
Year FE	No	Yes	Yes	No	Yes	Yes
Pair FE	No	No	Yes	No	No	Yes
Observations	27952	27952	27952	27952	27952	27952
Adjusted R^2	0.0002	0.030	0.066	0.001	0.025	0.061

Notes: * $p<0.1$; ** $p<0.05$; *** $p<0.01$. This table presents the empirical results of the second stage with cash policy dissimilarities as dependent variables. Definitions of the variables are provides in Appendix A.1.

TABLE 3.11 2nd. stage regression: reserve fund policy dissimilarities

	Dependent variable:					
	reserve fund policy dissimilarity					
	reserve. deposit			reserve. loan		
	(1)	(2)	(3)	(4)	(5)	(6)
BLS	-0.019*** (0.004)	-0.017*** (0.004)	-0.017*** (0.004)	-0.014*** (0.001)	-0.013*** (0.001)	-0.010*** (0.002)
agg. dir			-0.001*** (0.0002)			-0.001*** (0.0001)
agg. staff			0.00002*** (0.00001)			0.00001*** (0.00000)
agg. city			-0.00002 (0.00004)			-0.00002 (0.00001)
diff. asset		-0.003*** (0.001)	-0.003*** (0.001)		-0.001*** (0.0002)	-0.001*** (0.0002)
d iff. city		0.00000 (0.0001)	0.0001 (0.0001)		-0.00001 (0.00003)	0.0001* (0.00003)
d iff. staff		-0.00000 (0.00000)	-0.00002*** (0.00001)		-0.00000** (0.00000)	-0.00001*** (0.00000)

Continued

	Dependent variable:					
	reserve fund policy dissimilarity					
	reserve. deposit				reserve. loan	
	(1)	(2)	(3)	(4)	(5)	(6)
diff. RoE		-0.109*** (0.007)	-0.118*** (0.007)		-0.013*** (0.003)	-0.024*** (0.003)
same. type		0.004** (0.002)	0.005*** (0.002)		-0.009*** (0.001)	-0.009*** (0.001)
Constant	0.047*** (0.001)			0.027*** (0.0003)	0.029*** (0.001)	
Year FE	No	Yes	Yes	No	Yes	Yes
Pair FE	No	No	Yes	No	No	Yes
Observations	23536	23536	23536	23536	23536	23536
Adjusted R^2	0.001	0.013	0.014	0.004	0.037	0.029

Notes: * $p < 0.1$; ** $p < 0.05$; *** $p < 0.01$. This table presents the empirical results of the second stage with reserve fund related policy dissimilarities as dependent variables. Definitions of the variables are provides in Appendix A.1. or reserve policy that are 1% to 2% (Table 3.1) more similar than for two unconnected firms.

3.5 Endogeneity and Further Tests

3.5.1 Controlling for homogeneity

In the main regression I find that bank pairs behaved similarly in terms of operational decisions if they were linked through interlock directorates, and the similarity was positively related to the number of shared directors. However, the result could be biased if director tended to sit on the boards of banks with analogous characteristics, so that the outcome is only a reflection of the likeness of the bank pair. I address this endogenous concern with two strategies. In section 3.5.1, I carry out an analysis of the the connections among bank pairs, showing that the interbank linkages were more likely to be established among banks with divergent characteristics rather than similar ones, suggesting that relevant interlocks were formed on a heterogeneous basis. Second, section 3.5.1 considers region effects by restricting firm pairs to those with different headquarter locations. The results remain significant for pairs without geographical proximity, indicating that shared directors had a separate impact from interactions between banks and their directors due to physical closeness.

3.5.1.1 The pattern of board connection

This section provides a detailed examination of the attributes of banks linked through interlocks. The intention is to compare banks across each company pair to evaluate whether their traits differ from each other in any significant way. I focus on a bank's asset (*size*) and established year (*age*), as these two variables were correlated with the firm's other major characteristics and may reflect a bank's governance and maturity to some extent[①].

Table 3.12 (Bank pair size and age statistics) presents a statistical summary of these values for the sample period. Panel A lists the average size and age of the bank pairs on average, while panel B shows the distribution of trait differences over pairs[②]. The pair structure becomes clearer when the results from both panels are combined. From panel A, the average size of bank pairs remained stable in the sample years. The mean of the natural logarithm of total assets is about 17.5. In contrast, the mean size difference of bank pairs fluctuates around 2.2 across four years, with a standard deviation between 1.6 to 1.8. The result shows that, while the average size of bank pair (real value without natural logarithm) is $CSD 39824784, one bank of a pair is statistically 9 times larger than than the other. I observe a similar pattern in terms of age as well—the average establishment year of the bank pairs is around 1926 with the difference being 8 years on average. This implies that for

---

① Nguyen, Hagendorff, and Eshraghi (2015) uses the natural logarithm of the book value of total assets to control for bank size. Acheson et al. (2016a) suggests the establishment year of a company to capture the maturity of the firm.

② For example, suppose a bank pair is comprised of Bank A and B, mathematically, the *size on average* = $\log\left(\frac{assetA + assetB}{2}\right)$, and the *age on average* = $\left(\frac{assetA + assetB}{2}\right)$. With the same logic, the banks pair in difference calculates the difference in size and age between Bank A and B, namely, *size in diff* = $\left| ln(asset\ A) - ln(asset\ B) \right|$ and *age in diff* = $\left| age\ A - age\ B \right|$.

Chapter 3 Corporate Policies Propagation Through Board Connection

most bank pairs it is the case that one bank was established before year 1928—a critical year to distinguish old and new financial institutions①, while the counterpart was founded afterwards.

TABLE 3.12   Bank pair size and age statistics

	1933		1934		1935		1936	
	size	est. year	size	est. year	size	est. year	size	est. year
Panel A: bank pair data on average								
Mean	17.3	1924	17.3	1926	17.5	1927	17.8	1927
Panel B: bank pair data in difference								
Mean	2.12	8.08	2.18	8.36	2.26	8.06	2.37	7.98
S.D.	1.62	6.65	1.69	6.96	1.74	6.68	1.79	6.51
Min	0	0	0	0	0	0	0	0
P25	0.82	3	0.81	3	0.88	2	0.9	2
Median	1.78	7	1.81	7	1.88	6	2	6
P75	3.11	12	3.22	12	3.29	12	3.4	12
Max	9.43	37	9.59	37	10.26	28	11	29

Notes: The table shows the bank pair summary statistics and comparison with regard to natural logarithm of asset size as well as the year of establish. Panel A lists the size and est. year on average of all possible bank pairs in my sample, whereas Panel B presents the difference - in - mean summary.

I also find narrative evidence connected to my data to support my inference. For instance, The Bank of Greater Asia, Ltd, a

---

① A brief background information about the Chinese political and economic environments is introduced in section 3.2.

commercial bank, was established in Shanghai by Jusun YOU, a successful merchant with an industrial background. Initially, the total number of staff was 60, with a shareholder equity of $CSD 500000 in year 1934. Using his social connections he invited the business elite to sit on the board. These people include Yuesheng DU and Jinsan WEI—the most prestigious businessmen in China, particularly in the banking sector. By sharing these directors with other financial institutions, the Bank of Greater Asia set up connections with the largest state-owned institution, the Bank of China, and the Shanghai Citizen's Commercial and Savings Bank, Ltd, one of the most renowned commercial banks from scratch. In this case, it turns out that the founder of the small young bank chose deliberately, rather than randomly, key directors from other institutions who can bring economic advantages to enhance the reputation and position of the bank in the financial sector[①].

Overall, connected pairs exhibit a heterogeneous linking pattern that individual banks tend to link with divergent counterparts differing in major characteristics. This outcome mitigates my concern that the main empirical results are driven by the endogeneity that directors tended to sit on boards of similar banks. Banks were actually more likely to interlock with heterogeneous banks as complements rather than sharing directors with similar peers.

---

① In the narrative, bank information are excerpted from Economic Research Office (1936), the directors information are from individual biography database—The Modern and Contemporary Persons Integrated Information System. For detail of the database, see http://mhdb.mh.sinica.edu.tw/mhpeople/index.php.

3.5.1.2 Controlling for region effects

Ma (2016) highlights that modern Chinese banks were heavily concentrated in major metropolitan areas, like Shanghai and Tianjing. The geographical proximity of their headquarters could potentially have influenced the corporate decision making of banks in the same region. For example, financial institutions in Shanghai might have been influenced by membership or interaction with a sector-wide industry association, the Shanghai Bankers' Association (SBA) (Xu 2000). Such interactions enabled by geographic proximity could be a factor that affected an individual bank's operational decision making.

I investigate the impact of region effects to confirm that my main empirical result is not driven by regionally homogeneous banks. The underlying assumption is that banks from different regions, for example Peking and Shanghai, were not conducting operations in a coordinated fashion so that the tendency of being the same with regard to business practice and firm traits is small. I do this by restricting the sample to bank pairs with headquarters in different cities. In this way, I evaluate bank pairs that were shaped by different economic environments without a possible coordinating effect of geographic proximity.

Table 3.13 (bond policy dissimilarities of bank pairs with different head-quarter locations) reports the results of the BLS impact on three bond-related policies for the sample of bank pairs with different headquarter locations. Despite the reduction in observations, I find BLS still predicts similar corporate policies for bank pairs connected over interlock directorates. Interestingly, the economic magnitude of the effect is larger in the reduced sample when compared to the fixed effect specifications from Table 3.9 (between 50% and 200% larger). Further, the coefficient of BLS in column (5) become statistically significant in contrast to the unrestricted sample regression in Table 3.9 because it rules out the concern that the estimate including pairs in the same city could be driven by unobserved factors that lead to a biased result[①]. Once the specification excludes the sample pairs within the same region, the coefficient of BLS becomes statistically significant. Table 3.14 (cash and reserve policy dissimilarities of bank pairs with different headquarter) displays the empirical results of the BLS impact on cash and reserve related policies. The coefficients of BLS are statistically significant across all specifications, and they are consistent with the facts reported in Table 3.13.

Overall, this outcome exhibits that boardroom connections through interlocks were more prominent as channels of information transmission and coordination between banks located in different regions. This is consistent with the existing literature on interlock directorates claiming that director sharing serves the inter-firm collusion, cooptation and intentional (unintentional) transmission of knowledge (Mizruchi 1996; Haunschild and Beckman 1998; Helmers, Patnam, and Rau 2017).

---

① The endogeneity of social networks and data limitation is a broad issue for all empirical work in this body of literature. This point of view is admitted and supported by existing studies, such as Braggion (2011) and Larcker, So, and Wang (2013). This paper is no exception.

TABLE 3.13 bond policy dissimilarities of bank pairs with different head-quarter locations

Dependent variable:

	bond. deposit		bond policy dissimilarity bond. loan		bond. SH	
	(1)	(2)	(3)	(4)	(5)	(6)
BLS	−0.027*** (0.005)	−0.024*** (0.005)	−0.054*** (0.007)	−0.053*** (0.008)	−0.036* (0.020)	−0.080*** (0.020)
agg. dir		0.0003*** (0.0001)		0.001*** (0.0002)		−0.004*** (0.0005)
agg. staff		−0.00002*** (0.00000)		−0.00003*** (0.00001)		0.0003*** (0.00002)
agg. city		−0.00002 (0.00003)		−0.00003 (0.0001)		−0.00001 (0.0001)
diff. asset	0.0001 (0.0005)	−0.001 (0.0005)	−0.003*** (0.001)	−0.004*** (0.001)	−0.002 (0.002)	0.008*** (0.002)
diff. city	−0.0001 (0.0001)	−0.00005 (0.0001)	−0.00003 (0.0001)	−0.0001 (0.0001)	0.002*** (0.0002)	0.002*** (0.0003)
diff. staff	−0.00000 (0.00000)	0.00002*** (0.00001)	0.00001** (0.00000)	0.00003*** (0.00001)	0.0001*** (0.00001)	−0.0002*** (0.00002)

Continued

	Dependent variable:					
	bond. deposit		bond policy dissimilarity bond. loan		bond. SH	
	(1)	(2)	(3)	(4)	(5)	(6)
diff. RoE	0.146***	0.151***	0.423***	0.436***	1.243***	1.182***
	(0.005)	(0.005)	(0.008)	(0.008)	(0.020)	(0.020)
same. type	−0.014***	−0.015***	−0.013***	−0.014***	0.023***	0.034***
	(0.001)	(0.001)	(0.002)	(0.002)	(0.006)	(0.006)
Year FE	Yes	Yes	Yes	Yes	Yes	Yes
Pair FE	No	Yes	No	Yes	No	Yes
Observations	17318	17318	17318	17318	17318	17318
Adjusted R^2	0.101	0.063	0.190	0.160	0.244	0.212
F Statistic	244.711***	131.192***	509.718***	368.009***	701.021***	518.038***

Notes: * $p<0.1$; ** $p<0.05$; *** $p<0.01$. This table reports the results of the BLS impact on three bond related policies for the sample of bank pairs with different headquarter locations. Definitions of the variables are provides in Appendix A.1.

TABLE 3.14 cash and reserve policy dissimilarities of bank pairs with different headquarter locations

Dependent variable:

	policy dissimilarities							
	cash and reserve				reserve. deposit	reserve. deposit	reserve. loan	reserve. loan
	cash. deposit	cash. deposit	cash. loan	cash. loan				
	(1)	(2)	(3)	(4)	(5)	(6)	(7)	(8)
BLS	-0.011** (0.005)	-0.014*** (0.005)	-0.061*** (0.016)	-0.095*** (0.016)	-0.030*** (0.007)	-0.032*** (0.007)	-0.020*** (0.003)	-0.021*** (0.003)
agg. dir		-0.003*** (0.0001)		-0.007*** (0.0003)		-0.001*** (0.0002)		-0.001*** (0.0001)
agg. staff		0.0001*** (0.00000)		0.0003*** (0.00001)		0.00003*** (0.00001)		0.00002*** (0.00000)
agg. city		-0.00002 (0.00003)		-0.00000 (0.0001)		-0.00004 (0.00004)		-0.00004** (0.00002)
diff. asset	-0.002*** (0.0004)	-0.001 (0.0005)	-0.006*** (0.001)	0.003** (0.001)	-0.002*** (0.001)	-0.001 (0.001)	-0.001*** (0.0003)	-0.001*** (0.0003)
diff. city	0.0001 (0.0001)	0.0002*** (0.0001)	0.001*** (0.0002)	0.001*** (0.0002)	-0.00002 (0.0001)	0.0001 (0.0001)	-0.0001* (0.00003)	0.00001 (0.00004)
diff. staff	0.00002*** (0.00000)	-0.00003*** (0.00001)	0.00003*** (0.00001)	-0.0002*** (0.00002)	-0.00001* (0.00000)	-0.00003*** (0.00001)	0.00000 (0.00000)	-0.00001*** (0.00000)

Continued

	Dependent variable:							
	cash and reserve				policy dissimilarities			
	cash. deposit		cash. loan		reserve. deposit		reserve. loan	
	(1)	(2)	(3)	(4)	(5)	(6)	(7)	(8)
diff. RoE	-0.069***	-0.098***	-0.220***	-0.316***	-0.068***	-0.080***	-0.012***	-0.022***
	(0.005)	(0.005)	(0.015)	(0.015)	(0.007)	(0.007)	(0.003)	(0.003)
same. type	-0.020***	-0.017***	-0.064***	-0.052***	-0.002	-0.001	-0.011***	-0.011***
	(0.001)	(0.001)	(0.004)	(0.004)	(0.002)	(0.002)	(0.001)	(0.001)
Constant	0.065***		0.165***		0.045***		0.031***	
	(0.002)		(0.006)		(0.003)		(0.001)	
Year FE	Yes	Yes	Yes	Yes	Yes	Yes	Yes	Yes
Pair FE	No	Yes	No	Yes	No	Yes	No	Yes
Observations	22294	22294	22294	22294	19160	19160	19160	19160
Adjusted R^2	0.064	0.056	0.032	0.062	0.021	0.011	0.041	0.029

Notes: * $p<0.1$; ** $p<0.05$; *** $p<0.01$. This table reports the results of the BLS impact on cash and bank reserve – related policies for the sample of bank pairs with different headquarter locations. Definitions of the variables are provides in Appendix A.1.

3.5.2 Interbank cooperation or corporate control?

Another plausible alternative causal explanation of the policy co-movement over interlock directorates is corporate control. Interlocks have been viewed by observers as a means of corporate control as early as Mariolis (1975). He argues that banks might be able to control a corporation through such mechanisms as stock ownership or board representation. In my context, the extent to which banks are linked with each other may simply highlight the presence of power of one bank over another as primary shareholder. If so, the policy similarity of bank pairs may be a reflection of decisions implemented by one bank under orders from the parent institute (Mizruchi 1996). This alternative interpretation may lead to a biased estimation of my analysis. For instance, financial institutions located in metropolises could be heavily impacted by the local authorities. The policy may be driven by the regional regulations. BLS could be correlated with some unobserved or omitted firm characteristics that are associated with shareholding between the bank pair. If an individual bank, which was a major stock holder of the other one, was able to exercise control over the other through board representation, my finding may simply capture an explicit imposition of policies rather than the effect of information diffusion through interlocks.

Due to data constraints, neither the relevant shareholders nor a strictly exogenous variable to rule out the underlying biased estimate[1]

---

[1] A brief background information about the Chinese political and economic environments is introduced in section 3.2.

are available. However, I can carry out a series of tests to explore whether my findings are likely to be driven by the alternative hypothesis by restricting the sample to bank pairs that consist of young banks only. The underlying assumption is that the corporate control is less likely to happen among immature financial institutions as they are much more likely to be controlled than to control another bank. In this sense, the subset of bank pairs restricts the sample as much as possible so that policy co-movement over bank pairs was not driven by corporate control. I begin by estimating the pair model introduced in section 3.4.1 with a subsample of bank pairs that consist of only of young banks. I classify a bank as young if it was established after year 1928, a key year to distinguish old and new financial institutions in the Chinese context[1], but since my findings may be sensitive to this definition, I check the robustness of my results using year 1929 and year 1930 as alternative thresholds as well.

Table 3.15 (Policy dissimilarity regression with subsample of young banks) reports the second stage estimation of the pair model for selective policy measures from each policy group[2]. Compared to the full sample regressions in section 3.4.2, the restriction causes the sample size to drop from over 20000 to a range from 1800 to 6000 bank-pair-year observations.

---

[1] The empirical outcomes are persistent over all seven measures, however, due to the space limitation, I only list the specifications of three measures, namely bond. deposit, cash. deposit, and reserve. loan.

[2] This point of view is support by an extensive literature, for example, Jackson, Rogers, and Zenou (2017).

Chapter 3 Corporate Policies Propagation Through Board Connection

TABLE 3.15 Policy dissimilarity regression with subsample of young banks

Dependent variable:

	bond. deposit			policy dissimilarity cash. deposit			reserve. loan		
	(1) >1928	(2) >1929	(3) >1930	(4) >1928	(5) >1929	(6) >1930	(7) >1928	(8) >1929	(9) >1930
BLS	−0.016** (0.006)	−0.016** (0.007)	−0.018** (0.007)	−0.017** (0.007)	−0.017** (0.009)	−0.022* (0.012)	−0.010** (0.004)	−0.009* (0.005)	−0.010* (0.006)
agg. dir	−0.001*** (0.0003)	−0.002*** (0.0003)	0.0002 (0.0004)	−0.002*** (0.0003)	−0.003*** (0.0003)	−0.004*** (0.001)	−0.0005*** (0.0002)	−0.001*** (0.0002)	−0.001*** (0.0003)
agg. staff	−0.00004 (0.00003)	0.0002*** (0.00004)	0.00001 (0.00004)	−0.00003 (0.00002)	−0.00005 (0.00004)	−0.00003 (0.0001)	0.00004** (0.00001)	0.0001* − (0.00002)	0.0001* − (0.00003)
agg. city	−0.0003 (0.0003)	−0.0003 (0.0003)	0.0003 (0.0004)	−0.0001 (0.0002)	−0.00001 (0.0003)	0.00003 (0.0004)	−0.0002 (0.0001)	−0.0002 (0.0002)	−0.0001 (0.0003)
diff. asset	0.005*** (0.002)	0.014*** (0.002)	0.017*** (0.002)	−0.008*** (0.001)	−0.010*** (0.002)	−0.012*** (0.002)	−0.005*** (0.001)	−0.004*** (0.001)	−0.006*** (0.001)
diff. city	−0.0004 (0.0005)	−0.0004 (0.001)	−0.001 (0.001)	0.002*** (0.0004)	0.001** (0.0005)	0.004*** (0.001)	−0.0003 (0.0003)	−0.0004 (0.0003)	0.0002 (0.001)

Continued

	bond. deposit			policy dissimilarity cash. deposit			reserve. loan		
	(1) >1928	(2) >1929	(3) >1930	(4) >1928	(5) >1929	(6) >1930	(7) >1928	(8) >1929	(9) >1930
diff. staff	0.00003 (0.00003)	-0.0002*** (0.00005)	-0.00003 (0.0001)	0.0002*** (0.00003)	0.0002*** (0.00005)	0.0001* (0.0001)	-0.00003* (0.00002)	-0.0001*** (0.00003)	-0.0001*** (0.00004)
same. type	-0.010*** (0.003)	-0.007* (0.004)	0.018*** (0.004)	-0.030*** (0.003)	-0.038*** (0.004)	-0.051*** (0.005)	-0.014*** (0.002)	-0.017*** (0.003)	-0.017*** (0.004)
diff. RoE	0.154*** (0.012)	0.221*** (0.015)	0.137*** (0.014)	-0.088*** (0.012)	-0.090*** (0.015)	-0.106*** (0.019)	-0.040*** (0.007)	-0.037*** (0.010)	-0.095*** (0.012)
Year FE	Yes	Yes	Yes	Yes	Yes	Yes	Yes	Yes	Yes
Pair FE	Yes	Yes	Yes	Yes	Yes	Yes	Yes	Yes	Yes
Observations	4172	3070	1880	6070	4684	3176	4196	3050	1862
Adjusted R^2	0.060	0.111	0.105	0.065	0.075	0.104	0.031	0.035	0.055

Notes: * $p < 0.1$; ** $p < 0.05$; *** $p < 0.01$. This table reports the second stage estimation of the pair model for selective policy measure from each policy group with subsample of young banks. As robustness, alternative definitions of young bank are used in the regressions (1928, 1929, and 1930). Dependent variable are displayed in header. Definitions of the variables are provides in Appendix A.1.

The coefficients of interest (BLS) are negative across all specifications with various definition of young banks while remaining statistically significant at 5% to 10% levels. Except for column (8), the magnitude of the coefficients increases as I raise the restriction of the immaturity definition. It suggests that boardroom connections lead to more similar corporate policies and that the peer impact on their own decisions was even stronger over bank pairs in which banks had been established after year 1930—a stricter definition of immaturity under that the alternative hypothesis is even more likely to be excluded. Taken together, this evidence is consistent with individual banks having been influenced in their corporate policies from their peers at board level rather than through a direct control structure.

3.6 Bank Network and Operational Policies

I show above that interbanking connections had an reciprocal influence on corporate policies, when examined on a bank pair basis. However, as Figure 3.1 shows, an individual bank was not only linked with another bank, but embedded in the boardroom network of the whole sector. If banks had an impact on each other, the next logical step is that the global position of an individual bank in the network also influences its corporate policy. Based on this idea, I conduct an analysis to confirm whether and how that global position of an individual bank in the boardroom network influenced its corporate policy making.

3.6.1 Analysis framework

The analysis in this section is inspired by the literature on information diffusion in corporate networks. Larcker, So, and Wang (2013) argue that directors on a board possess a wealth of information on industry trends, market conditions, and extra key data if they are well-connected through social networks. Thus, someone in a central position in an inter-firm network may have better access to such information and therefore have a comparative advantage in corporate decision making (Mol 2001), especially as central players are more exposed to word-of-mouth and internal information (Fracassi 2017). Based on these arguments, I expect that banks' strategic decisions reflect private information from their peers more strongly if they were connected with more banks. On the opposite side, this postulates that isolated banks lack access to these resources from the network conduit, and thus are expected to behave in a more idiosyncratic way.

This section examines the idea that the corporate policy decisions of the modern Chinese banks were affected by the location of the corporation in the inter-firm network. According to the mechanism above, banks located in a central position of the network were capable of collecting signals from their social peers. The received signals then shaped an individual bank's adoption of corporate strategies. The actual decision of a corporation, consequently, should reflect the extent to which a bank received information from its peers, in other words, its corporate policy reveals partly the position of a bank in the network. I therefore expect that more central banks had less unique policies compared to less connected ones.

I follow Fracassi (2017) in using a two-stage econometric model to examine the relationship between corporate policy decisions and network location in the Chinese context. My estimating equation takes the form:

First stage:

$$Policy\ measure_{i,t} = \alpha_0 + \alpha_1 Control_{Pi,t} + FE_i + FE_t + \varepsilon_{i,t}; \quad (3.4)$$

Second stage:

$$\log(1 + |\varepsilon_{i,t}|) = \beta_0 + \beta_1 Connectedness_{i,t} + \beta_2 Contol_{Ci,t} + \eta_{i,t}. \quad (3.5)$$

I use the corporate policies from section 3.3.2 as dependent variables at the first stage. The *Policy measure*$_{i,t}$ is regressed on common controls, e.g., bank age, size, board characteristics including the time and individual fixed effects. This first stage is similar to the one introduced in section 3.4.1. I then define an indicator to measure the idiosyncratic behavior of bank i at time t, which is the natural logarithm of $(1 + |\varepsilon_{i,t}|)$ in equation 3.5. *Connectedness*$_{i,t}$ stands for the connectedness measure of an individual bank, which evaluates how central a bank is in a network, and is described in more detail later on.

Equation 3.5 investigates the correlation between a bank's network position and its idiosyncratic behavior. Based on the hypothesis mentioned above, I expect the coefficient β_1 to be negative, indicating that a more centrally located bank exhibited less idiosyncratic behavior as the result of more access to signals and information from its peers.

3.6.2 Bank connectedness measure

I adopt two centrality indicators commonly used in the social network literature to measure the position of a bank in the boardroom network[①]. The most basic measure of centrality is called Degree. It is the number of links a node has with other nodes. Degree illuminates the relative importance of actors, banks, within the network, and can have practical consequences. For example, in terms of information contagion, an actor who is linked with a larger number of other actors is likely to receive external messages differently, potentially more frequently and faster than actors that are relatively isolated in the network through a lower number of links (Lamberson 2016). In a network of interlocking directorates, the degree measure shows for each bank with how many other banks it shares a director, so has an interlocking directorate. A bank may be well-connected if it possesses more channels of communications or resource exchange.

In addition to examining the direct connections of the nodes, I am also interested in how close each one is to every other node in the network. This idea leads to the second concept of Closeness centrality. The Closeness centrality measure attempts to capture the notion that a node is "central" if it is "close" to many other nodes. In the

---

① The existing literature on social network often use four measures to indicate the centrality of the players, for instance, Jackson (2009) and Larcker, So, and Wang (2013). The four centrality measures are: degree, closeness, betweenness, and eigenvector. For a detail description of the measure, see Jackson (2010). In my data, however, I do find a high correlation among these measures, therefore I only utilize two of them.

Chapter 3 Corporate Policies Propagation Through Board Connection

corporate context, if an actor has comparatively closer ties to more boards, it facilitates better information diffusion and exchange to this node (Larcker, So, and Wang 2013). As more central actors can quickly interact with many other boards across the network, these nodes find it easier to profit from the benefits of these connections. Banks with higher Closeness values are engaging in more exchange of information, which allows them to operate more profitably as well as develop a better understanding of the outside environment. The easier information access implies an advantage for these banks also in the way they are able to react to changes in an unstable political and economic environment[1].

In Appendix A.2, I provide the mathematical definition of both measures and calculation examples that help readers to capture the concept.

3.6.3 Empirical outcomes

The empirical results do not provide any statistical evidence regarding the relationship between bond – related policies and corporate idiosyncratic behavior. One possible reason is a noisy measurement of idiosyncratic behavior in these policies. However, I do find strong evidence when I replace bond – related policies with cash and reserve policies of banks, consequently this section focuses[2]

---

[1] Recent studies confirm the information spillover of boardroom network as well as other social connections among firms, for example, Helmers, Patnam, and Rau (2017), Hochberg, Ljungqvist, and Lu (2007) and Gao et al. (2012).

[2] For brevity, the section also skips listing the result of the first stage regression, since it resembles the first stage outcome in Table 3.8.

on these particular outcomes.

Table 3.16 (Bank board connectedness and idiosyncratic policies) reports the econometric results of the second stage. The dependent variable is the idiosyncratic behavior of a corporation across all columns, as defined in equation 3.5. I control for firm size and common characteristics of the banks, as in the prior pair model. In particular, previous literature suggests the relationship between performance and corporate variables may be non–linear (McConnell and Servaes 1990; Acheson et al. 2016a). That centrality measures I use in the regression could be correlated with firm's performance implies that the relationship between my main variables (*degree* and *closeness*) and the dependent variable (corporate idiosyncratic behavior) could be non–linear as well. I include a squared term—In ($assets^2$) to address this.

The connectedness coefficient (coefficient of *degree* and *closeness*) is negative across all specifications and statistically significant except for the last two columns concerning the *reserve deposit* policy. Overall, I find strong evidence that banks with more connections had less unique or idiosyncratic cash and reserve fund policies, even if the reserve deposit specifications remain insignificant. These results provide at least some support for my hypothesis that interbank connections influenced banks not only locally at an individual level, but also at the network level. The empirical results are consistent with Fracassi (2017), suggesting that companies have less idiosyncratic corporate policies once they retain more social ties.

The econometric framework was not designed to prove causality. Consequently, there may be unobserved factors that jointly caused an

TABLE 3.16 Bank board connectedness and idiosyncratic policies

Dependent variable: corporate idiosyncratic behavior

	cash. deposit		cash. loan		reserve. loan		reserve.	deposit
	(1)	(2)	(3)	(4)	(5)	(6)	(7)	(8)
degree	-0.001* (0.0004)		-0.005*** (0.001)		-0.001*** (0.0003)		-0.001 (0.001)	
closeness		-2.506** (1.151)		-9.441*** (3.214)		-1.376** (0.593)		-0.327 (1.537)
ln(assets)	0.000 (0.000)	0.000 (0.000)	0.000 (0.000)	0.000 (0.000)	0.000** (0.000)	0.000** (0.000)	0.000 (0.000)	0.000 (0.000)
ln(assets"2)	0.003** (0.001)	0.003** (0.001)	0.016*** (0.003)	0.015*** (0.003)	0.002*** (0.001)	0.002*** (0.001)	0.002 (0.002)	0.002 (0.001)
board size	-0.003*** (0.001)	-0.003*** (0.001)	-0.005** (0.002)	-0.006*** (0.002)	-0.001 (0.0004)	-0.001*** (0.0004)	-0.0002 (0.001)	-0.001 (0.001)
#staff	0.00003 (0.00002)	0.00003 (0.00002)	0.00001 (0.0001)	-0.00001 (0.0001)	-0.00002* (0.00001)	-0.00002** (0.00001)	-0.00001 (0.00003)	-0.00001 (0.00003)
#city	-0.0004 (0.0004)	-0.0004 (0.0004)	-0.001 (0.001)	-0.001 (0.001)	0.0001 (0.0002)	0.0001 (0.0002)	0.0001 (0.0005)	0.0001 (0.0005)

Continued

	Dependent variable: corporate idiosyncratic behavior							
	cash. deposit		cash. loan		reserve. loan		reserve. deposit	
	(1)	(2)	(3)	(4)	(5)	(6)	(7)	(8)
if. connected	-0.004	0.010	0.025	0.064**	0.011***	0.014**	0.009	0.006
	(0.008)	(0.011)	(0.022)	(0.031)	(0.004)	(0.006)	(0.011)	(0.015)
Year FE	Yes	Yes	Yes	Yes	Yes	Yes	Yes	Yes
Pair FE	Yes	Yes	Yes	Yes	Yes	Yes	Yes	Yes
Observations	433	433	433	433	405	405	405	405
R^2	0.107	0.112	0.111	0.105	0.093	0.072	0.015	0.012
F Statistic	6292***	6621***	6573***	6149***	5.044***	3791***	0.768	0.576

Notes: * $p < 0.1$; ** $p < 0.05$; *** $p < 0.01$. This table reports the regression result of the idiosyncratic behavior model. Two network centrality measures are used in the analysis, namely degree and closeness. Details of the network centrality measure refer to Section 3.6.2. Definitions of the variables are provides in Appendix A.1.

Chapter 3 Corporate Policies Propagation Through Board Connection

individual bank's position in the network and its idiosyncratic strategies. For instance, a bank that choose to establish connections with peers may select a major metropolis, such as Shanghai, in which to locate its headquarters[1]. Giving a higher level of information sharing in that location, especially through the local industry association, Shanghai Bankers' Association (SBA, Xu 2000), that decision could have had a joint impact on both network position and the idiosyncratic behavior. There may also be issues, for instance, in whether the connectedness measure used in the analysis is the appropriate proxy to capture the centrality of a bank. These issues mean to indicate ultimately, the most that I can say about any relationships are that they are correlations, and do not necessarily imply causality.

3.7 Why did Banks Coordinate Their Corporate Policy?

Above I demonstrated that interlocking directorates were linked with the co-movement of corporate policies between pairs of banks, suggesting that board connections between two banks lead to the transfer of internal information and result in more similar operational strategies. However, this does not address the incentives or benefits of this seeming coordination. This section explores the benefits and

---

[1] Kong and Ploeckl (2018a) offers an discussion of the factors driving establishment of connections.

implications of banks' social connections through the board network, and investigates whether being in a central position in the network was linked not only with less idiosyncratic, but also better decisions.

3.7.1 The profitability effect of being connected

A natural extension is to examine whether the corporate policies I test were associated with banks' profitability. If that is the case, the co-movement of these strategic choices is an indication that the implicit coordination of banks' operational policies through board connections was another mechanism through which banks enhanced their profitability.

Consequently, I investigate the correlation between the economic performance of a firm, measured by ROE and profit per capita, and the corporate policies I use in the prior analysis. I define the the return on equity as the ratio of annual net profit over total assets, and the profit per capita as the ratio of the net profit over the staff number of the individual bank.

Table 3.17 (Correlation between corporate policies and ROE) and Table 3.18 (Correlation between corporate policies and profit per capita) highlight the main results of the regressions of ROE and profit per capita over various corporate policies after controlling for common factors used in the existing literature[①]. In terms of bond-related policies, I find a positive and significant correlation with ROE. All of the three bond measures demonstrate a high level of co-movement with ROE, statistically, as shown in columns (1) to (3) of Table

---

① For example, Acheson et al. (2016a) and Campbell and Turner (2011).

3.17. In contrast, the relationship is not that close between bond policy and profit per capita. However, the coefficient of bond/deposit ratio remains highly significant in the regression on profit per capita, as shown in Column (1) of Table 3.18. With regard to cash and reserve policies, I do not observe any statistical correlations between the measures and ROE [column (4) to (7) of Table 3.17]. This implies that the coordination of cash and reserve operations among bank pairs may not have been motivated by pursuing a higher ROE. Yet column (4) to (6) of Table 3.18 demonstrate strong relationships of these policy measures with profit per capita, suggesting again that the cash and reserve decisions of individual banks, such as their bond policies, had strong ties to their profitability.

Overall, I find positive and significant relationships between my policy measures and banks' economic performance. This finding provides a reasonable motivation for the corporate policy co-movement among bank pairs that modern Chinese banks coordinated or imitated the bond/cash/reserve related corporate policies of their peers to achieve better performance, which I call the profitability effect of the board ties. It is well worth stressing that the empirical result is only suggestive of a relationship between my policy measures and profitability, but is not proof of a causal relation between the two[1]. I, therefore, can not conclude that the policy measures I use in the article caused any change of banks' ROA and profit per capita.

---

[1] Chapter 4 offers an insight into the investigation that higher centrality was connected to a higher profitability.

TABLE 3.17 Correlation between corporate policies and ROE

	Dependent variable: ROE						
	(1)	(2)	(3)	(4)	(5)	(6)	(7)
bond. deposit	0.061** (0.030)						
bond. loan		0.044** (0.020)					
bond. SH			0.017*** (0.003)				
cash. deposit				-0.019 (0.090)			
cash. loan					-0.016 (0.033)		
reserve. loan						-0.164 (0.271)	
reserve. deposit							-0.043 (0.070)
ln (assets)	0.017*** (0.004)	0.016*** (0.004)	0.012*** (0.004)	0.036** (0.014)	0.037** (0.015)	0.037** (0.015)	0.037** (0.015)

Continued

	Dependent variable: ROE						
	(1)	(2)	(3)	(4)	(5)	(6)	(7)
board size	−0.004***	−0.004***	−0.004***	−0.005	−0.005	−0.005	−0.005
	(0.001)	(0.001)	(0.001)	(0.005)	(0.005)	(0.005)	(0.005)
#staff	−0.00001	−0.00001	−0.00001	−0.0001	−0.0001	−0.0001	−0.0001
	(0.00002)	(0.00002)	(0.00002)	(0.0001)	(0.0001)	(0.0001)	(0.0001)
#cities	0.0002	0.0001	0.0002	0.002	0.002	0.002	0.002
	(0.001)	(0.001)	(0.001)	(0.002)	(0.002)	(0.002)	(0.002)
if. connected	0.002	0.004	−0.005	−0.082*	−0.082*	−0.083	−0.082
	(0.012)	(0.012)	(0.011)	(0.048)	(0.047)	(0.050)	(0.050)
Year FE	Yes	Yes	Yes	Yes	Yes	Yes	Yes
Pair FE	Yes	Yes	Yes	Yes	Yes	Yes	Yes
Observations	396	396	396	433	433	405	405
Adjusted R^2	0.110	0.112	0.168	0.021	0.022	0.022	0.022

Notes: * $p<0.1$; ** $p<0.05$; *** $p<0.01$. This table demonstrates the correlations between the bank profitability measured by RoE and different policy indicators in each column. Definitions of the variables are provides in Appendix A.1.

TABLE 3.18 Correlation between corporate policies and profit per capita

	Dependent variable: Ln (profit per capita)						
	(1)	(2)	(3)	(4)	(5)	(6)	(7)
bond. deposit	0.939*** (0.358)						
bond. loan		0.316 (0.238)					
bond. SH			-0.041 (0.037)				
cash. deposit				0.701*** (0.232)			
cash. loan					0.163* (0.086)		
reserve. loan						1.789*** (0.675)	
reserve. deposit							-0.251 (0.177)
ln (assets)	0.342*** (0.042)	0.333*** (0.043)	0.354*** (0.044)	0.349*** (0.037)	0.354*** (0.038)	0.356*** (0.038)	0.366*** (0.038)

Continued

	\multicolumn{7}{c}{Dependent variable: Ln (profit per capita)}						
	(1)	(2)	(3)	(4)	(5)	(6)	(7)
board size	0.019 (0.013)	0.021 (0.013)	0.021 (0.013)	0.022* (0.012)	0.021* (0.012)	0.025** (0.012)	0.022* (0.012)
#staff	-0.001*** (0.0002)	-0.001*** (0.0002)	-0.001*** (0.0002)	-0.001*** (0.0002)	-0.001*** (0.0002)	-0.001*** (0.0002)	-0.001*** (0.0002)
#cities	-0.012* (0.006)	-0.011* (0.006)	-0.011* (0.006)	-0.010* (0.006)	-0.011* (0.006)	-0.012** (0.006)	-0.012** (0.006)
if . connected	-0.075 (0.138)	-0.029 (0.137)	0.019 (0.139)	-0.001 (0.123)	-0.051 (0.122)	-0.041 (0.126)	-0.052 (0.127)
Year FE	Yes	Yes	Yes	Yes	Yes	Yes	Yes
Pair FE	Yes	Yes	Yes	Yes	Yes	Yes	Yes
Observations	396	396	396	433	433	405	405
Adjusted R²	0.170	0.159	0.158	0.222	0.212	0.221	0.211

Notes: * p < 0.1; ** p < 0.05; *** p < 0.01. This table demonstrates the correlations between the bank profitability measured by natural logarithm of profit per capita (in Chinese dollar) and different policy indicators in each column. Definitions of the variables are provides in Appendix A.1.

But the test provides a potential mechanism to explain the causality between network centrality and banks' economic performance discussed in Chapter 4.

3.7.2 The insurance effect of being connected

China experienced political and economic turbulence during the 1930s. The banking sector, which usually relies strongly on the security of property rights and contract enforcement (Ma 2016), was particular sensitive to an uncertain environment. In this part, I therefore follow a similar two-stage model introduced in Section 3.6 to investigate whether being connected results from banks' intention to seek assurance and eliminate risk.

In the first step of the model, a bank i's profitability measure at time t is regressed on the conventional control variables Controlpit with time and individual fixed effects. I construct an indicator, as $\log(1 + |\varepsilon_{i,t}|)$, to measure the excess fluctuation of profitability that can not be explained by controls or the predictor variables. This *Profitability measure* incorporates ROE and the natural logarithm of profit per capita. The second stage of the model tests whether a correlation exists between the connectedness of an individual bank i and its excess fluctuation. As network connectedness indicators, I adopt the same measures, namely degree and closeness, as introduced above in Section 3.6.2. This two-stage model can be described mathematically as:

First stage:

$$\Pr ofitability\ measure_{i,t} = \alpha_0 + \alpha_1 Control_{Pi,t} + FE_i + FE_t + \varepsilon_{i,t};$$

(3.6)

Chapter 3 Corporate Policies Propagation Through Board Connection

Second stage:

$$\log(1+|\varepsilon_{i,t}|) = \beta_0 + \beta_1 Connectedness_{i,t} + \beta_2 Contol_{Ci,t} + \eta_{i,t}. \quad (3.7)$$

The idea is that the model compares the profitability excess fluctuation of banks with more board connections to those with less links. If a statistically significant difference of excess fluctuation is observed between the two groups, that suggests that the connectedness of a bank had an impact on the fluctuation of its profitability, which, in turn, indicates that the motivation of a financial institution to establish board connections was influenced by risk concerns.

Equation 3.6 illustrates the idea mathematically: the *profitability* volatility of individual bank i can be predicted by factors included in *control* plus the random part stocked in the residual ε_i. By eliminating the unpredicted part in the residual, banks could potentially minimize the profitability volatility risk from uncertainty.

Table 3.19 (The second stage regression of the profitability excess fluctuation) presents the results of the second stage regression[①]. I break down the results by profitability measure using ROE (columns 1 and 2) and the natural logarithm of profit per capita (columns 3 and 4) in the first stage. In all specifications, the coefficients of interest, bank centrality measure degree and closeness, are negative, indicating that stronger board connections leads to a less fluctuation than was indicated by the residuals from the first stage.

---

① Due to the space limitation, the empirical outcome of the first stage is not listed and can be provided on request.

TABLE 3.19 The second stage regression of the profitability excess fluctuation

	Dependent variable: Excess fluctuation RoE ln (profit per capita)			
	(1)	(2)	(3)	(4)
degree closeness	-0.001** (0.0003)	-1.966*** (0.735)	-0.005** (0.003)	-10.582* (5.629)
ln (assets)	0.006*** (0.001)	0.005*** (0.001)	-0.00004 (0.011)	-0.003 (0.011)
board size	-0.001** (0.001)	-0.001*** (0.0005)	0.001 (0.004)	-0.0003 (0.004)
#staff	-0.00000 (0.00001)	-0.00001 (0.00001)	-0.00000 (0.0001)	-0.00004 (0.0001)
#city	0.0003 (0.0002)	0.0003 (0.0002)	0.001 (0.002)	0.001 (0.002)
If. connected	-0.007 (0.005)	0.004 (0.007)	0.008 (0.040)	0.056 (0.057)
Year FE	Yes	Yes	Yes	Yes
Bank FE	Yes	Yes	Yes	Yes
Observations	289	289	289	289
Adjusted R^2	0.089	0.098	0.015	0.014

Notes: * $p<0.1$; ** $p<0.05$; *** $p<0.01$. This table shows the empirical result of the second stage regression of the profitability excess fluctuation. Definitions of the variables are provides in Appendix A.1.

A possible economic interpretation of the results is that the inter-bank board connections helped reduce the risk and, in turn, weakened the excess fluctuation of profitability. Establishing board connections was therefore likely influenced and motivated by banks seeking less volatility in their profitability, which resembles an insurance effect.

To illustrate this, I confirm this insurance argument by demonstrating the first stage residual distribution of regressions (namely, $\varepsilon_{i,t}$ in Equation 3.6) using ln ($profit\ per\ capita$) as predicted variable in Figure 3.2 (Residual distribution of the profit per capita regression). Banks with degree greater than 8 are classified as ones with high connections[①]. Corporations without any board ties are shown as comparison. The residual distributions of regressions in both

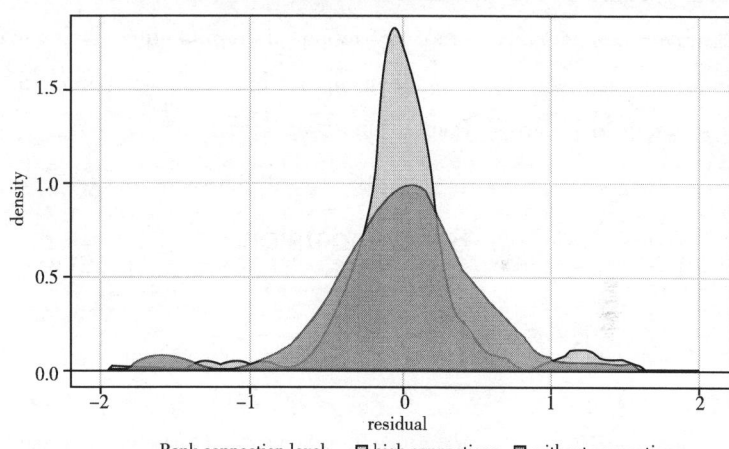

Bank connection level: ☐ high connections ☐ without connection

FIGURE 3.2 Residual distribution of the profit per capita regression

Notes: The density plot demonstrates the residual of the first stage regression derived from Equation 3.6. The plot in red represents the residual density distribution of banks with board connections greater than 8. In contrast, the blue colored plot highlights the residual distribution of banks without any board connection.

---

① Banks with $degree$ of 8 or more cover approximately 30% of the full sample. Alternative classifications did not significantly change the final results.

categories show a significant difference in shape, though both peak at zero. For banks with more connections, the value of residuals is more stacked at zero, showing less profitability volatility risk from uncertainty. Correspondingly, the excess fluctuation is smaller. In contrast, the group without links presents a broader residual distribution, or in other words, banks without board connections experienced a higher excess fluctuation with regard to profit per capita.

Overall, the visual evidence is consistent with the argument that being connected was associated with banks' intentions to seek assurance and eliminate risk in terms of profitability. "Staying connected" is likely to help the modern Chinese banks reduce the idiosyncratic risk derived from an uncertain environment.

3.8 Conclusion

Social and economic networks are one of the central features in corporate finance (Larcker, So, and Wang 2013; Jackson, Rogers, and Zenou 2017). I explore how the board connections of a bank within the interbank network affected its corporate policy decisions in a historical context. The results show that corporate decisions of banks were influenced by their social peers in that the more directors two banks shared with each other, the more similar were their corporate strategies. After establishing that firm policies were influenced by immediate network neighbors, I investigate further whether the global position of an individual bank in the network had any impact on its strategic decision makings. The analysis shows that banks with a central position in the boardroom network made corporate decisions more in line with the sector at large. The result highlights that peer behavior affects firms' own decisions not only at the bilateral level but network – wide.

In addition, the empirical outcome shows that co – moving corporate policies were positively related with banks' economic performance, suggesting that banks acted in a seemingly coordinated fashion with each other at the board level to achieve better performance and interlocking directorates were a critical channel for sharing managerial practices. Besides the level of performance the coordinating effect of these connections was also linked to a lower volatility of bank profitability, indicating an insurance effect reducing idiosyncratic risk for banks.

My findings yield important implications for understanding social networking in corporate finance. I clearly show that the boardroom network can be an essential conduit of influence and information flows that affect the strategic decision making of firms in the network. Modern Chinese bank data in the 1930s, the analysis also suggests that social connections are likely to be a useful tool to coordinate firms in politically and economically risky environments. Further research on China that explores social connections between financial institutions and industries can potentially provide insights into the mechanism of information passing through social networks and the role played by modern banks in connections with the economic development and political unification of the country.

Connections and Performance: The Impact of Interlocking Directorates

The Chinese modern banking industry had become the vanguard of growth in the Republican time period (from year 1910 to year 1949), in which property rights and contract enforcement were a luxuries. I examine whether one type of interbanking connections, namely interlocking directorate, contributed to the overall performance of Chinese modern banks by utilizing the social network tools. I find characteristics of banks, which share directors with other banks, are significantly different compared to those of unconnected counterparts. The empirical results elucidate a high positive correlation between bank's profitability and its connections with rivals through interlocking directors. The outcome provides a reasonable explanation about the success of

Chapter 4 Connections and Performance: The Impact of Interlocking Directorates Chinese banking sector in the 1930s.

4.1 Introduction

The modern Chinese banking industry became the vanguard of growth in the so - called Nanjing decade (from year 1927 to year 1937), a time of political and economic turbulence. This external uncertainty led the sector to be characterized by cooperation rather than competition as discussed in Chapter 2. A formal interbank network, based on sharing directors, reflected the strong social connections among bankers, who formed an elite social group of Chinese society driving economic development[1]. But did the relationships between banks serve more than just defensive purposes and actually positively impact the involved banks' performance? The question remains unanswered in the existing studies on Chinese financial history.

This paper, consequently, contributes to current research by examining whether interlocking directorates, as an explicit form of interbank linkages, were an important force leading to an improved performance of modern banks during the height of the Nanjing decade

---

[1] Bergere (1989) analyzes the effects of the rising Chinese bourgeoisie, and summarizes that bankers, as an elite class, were a leading group driving Chinese society's changes in general. Cheng (2003) confirms this assertion and argues that the success of banking sector was attributed to a group of entrepreneurs with Chinese characteristics. These bankers, as an elite social group, were the main force driving the expansion of modern Chinese banks. Consequently, Lan (2014) highlights the interrelations among bankers, formed in various ways like common location of origin, education, employment or entrepreneurial activity, promoted cooperation between banks.

from year 1933 to year 1936. I assert that these prevalent connections among banks served as a network of interbanking cooperation, that positively impacted the financial performance of the involved enterprises. The shape of the network highlights differences in the importance and centrality of the involved banks. Directors of banks with a more central position in this network could get more access to relevant information and resources and consequently were able to improve their banks' daily operations[①]. Bankers closer to the core of the network could use their social status and capital, expertise, and connections to influence corporate policies and board decisions and therefore enhance the performance of their well-connected banks (Fracassi 2017).

I build annual interbank networks based on interlocking directorates from year 1933 to year 1936 to examine the relationship between board connections and cooperation performance. In these networks the nodes represent individual banks while the edges are boardroom connections based on shared directors. For each year I then calculate measures of each bank's well-connectedness in the corresponding boardroom network and test their relationships with the economic performance as reflected by Return on Assets (ROE) and Profit per staff member.

I use four centrality measures derived from social network analysis (SNA) to capture an individual bank's position in the

---

[①] Existing literature as early as Mizruchi (1996) highlighted the importance of social connections in corporate operation and their impact on economic outcome. Recent studies, e.g. Larcker, So, and Wang (2013), Nguyen, Hagendorff, and Eshraghi (2015), provide convincing econometric evidence to support the point of view.

boardroom network. The first and most basic indicator is *degree centrality*. The degree of a node is the number of direct connections that involve that node. The idea of *degree centrality* is that a bank may be well-connected if it possesses more channels of communications and resource exchange. This measure offers a basic starting point of how to measure the board ties of an individual bank. Next, a board may be well connected if it keeps closer relations with other banks throughout the whole sector, which is captured by the *closeness centrality* measure. Similarly, a bank is located in a more central position if it sits in an intermediary position between other banks, thereby serving as a communications conduit between other boards. This is measured by betweenness centrality. Lastly, I use *eigenvector centrality* to capture the point that a node is more important if it is linked to other important nodes.

The annual inter-bank networks from 1933 to 1936, which are used in the empirical analysis, are based on the board compositions of 209 Chinese banks involving 3060 individuals. This information has been collected from the Bank Annual (1934 – 1937), an official record of annual financial statistics. This is also the main source for the banks' accounting data used in the analysis. Further director level data, such as middle name, birthplace, and age, which are used to help identify individual managers, have been collected from various biographies and related sources[1].

---

[1] The main biographical source I use in this study is an online open database called the Modern and Contemporary Persons Integrated Information System. This database contains various biographies of individuals who worked in the banking sector. For detail of the database, see http://mhdb.mh.sinica.edu.tw/mhpeople/index.php.

The empirical analysis initially exhibits an ambiguous results for estimations linking performance and centrality measures. *Closeness centrality* was statistically correlated with banks' performance, for both ROA and profit per staff measures. In contrast, however, I find no significant relationship between network location and performance of banks once I replace *closeness centrality* with *degree*, *betweenness* and *eigenvector centrality* as alternative network position indicators. To better understand this differentiation between closeness and the other network centrality measures, I conduct a principal component analysis (PCA) on the centrality measures. The purpose of PCA is to look at the relative appropriateness and explanatory power of these centrality measures, and the underlying relationships between the four network indicators. The outcome of the analysis suggests that *closeness* did indeed significantly differ from the other three indicators in measuring individual banks' positions, suggesting that this measure reflected certain structures that had a substantial relevance for the performance of modern Chinese banks.

Overall, the empirical outcome offers evidence that a more central location within the sector as measured by the *closeness centrality* network measure was associated with a better financial performance. Economically, my results imply that it were domestic Chinese banks with relatively closer links to outside boards all over the sector, rather than the number of links or intermediary role, that profited from more information and faster resource exchange, associated with higher returns and profits.

I provide additional support for these results with set of robust tests and further exploration of the data. First, I start by documenting a basic statistical correlation between "connectedness" and profitability of financial institutions with a difference – in – means test between banks with and without busy directors, those that were members of multiple boards. The outcome shows *profit per staff* for banks with at least one busy directors was statistically and economically greater than that of banks without. The result holds after a propensity – score matching (PSM), which avoids the issue of bank heterogeneity in the comparison.

Next, I use an alternative measure of board well – connectedness, namely board busyness, which is defined as the ratio between the number of directors in an interlocking directorate and overall board size of an individual bank. I test whether board connectedness measure in this way and bank performance were related. The econometric results are consistent with the results of the main analysis, showing that a higher share of interlocking directors in a board leads to greater profitability, both in ROA and profit per staff member. This result, again, supports the prediction that busy directors acted as conduits to facilitate the exchange of resources and information, thereby contributing further value to their financial institutions.

Further, I carry out a network neighborhood analysis to explore the pattern of an individual bank's links. Specifically, I measure the attributes of network neighborhood banks, the other banks to which an individual financial institution was linked, and evaluate whether a systematic linkage pattern existed. The analysis shows that the most – connected banks statistically tended to be connected with banks who held more assets, and neighbor banks are those more likely with higher leverage and lower liquidity. The results imply that interlocking with bigger and stronger institutions likely offered potential economic benefits, which shed light on the functions of interlocking directorates in an uncertain environment.

As the final point, I conduct a test to explore the potential endogeneity issues for the main econometric analysis. I restrict the sample to banks whose board composition remained unchanged from the previous period to the current year and examine the correlation between their board centrality and future economic consequences. The resulting evidence from these tests shows that it is unlikely that the main results are driven by interlocking directors being attracted to banks that were performing better in the future, providing indicative evidence against a potential endogeneity effect.

The rest of the article is organized as follows. Section 4.2 offers the historical backgrounds. Section 4.3 presents the modelling approach, describes the construction of the data set, conducts the main empirical analysis and discusses the main findings. In Section 4.4 I conduct several robust tests and further data explorations as well as an investigation into potential endogeneity. Section 4.5 concludes the paper.

4.2 Historical Background

4.2.1 The modern Chinese banking industry in the Republican period

The first Chinese modern domestic bank was established in year

Chapter 4 Connections and Performance: The Impact of Interlocking Directorates

1897, more than half a century after a British bank had set up its first branch in China. From the fall of the Qing Dynasty in year 1911 forwards, China was caught in the period of the warlords. During the time span of political turbulence from year 1912 to year 1927, a total of 266 new banks opened for business, around 18 each year. Almost half of them, however, went out of business during the same period①.

After the warlord era ended with the establishment of the Nationalist government in Nanjing in year 1927, the so-called Nanjing decade (from year 1927 to year 1937) began. Indeed, the total paid-up capital of Chinese banks increased from C$167② million in year 1927 to C$403 million in year 1936. From year 1927 to year 1936, modern Chinese banks more than doubled their capital and reserve funds, tripled their loans and total assets, and quadrupled their deposits③. Table 4.1 (Chinese modern bank statistics from year 1896 to year 1937) presents the Chinese modern bank statistics from year 1896 to year 1937. The number of banks raised rapidly, particularly after the establishment of the Nationalist government in Nanjing in year 1927. By June 1937, the total quantity of Chinese modern banks crept up to 164.

---

① Based on the study of Cheng (2003).
② C$ = Chinese Yuan.
③ These figures are from Bank of China, National banking year book, 1937. and Cheng (2003).

TABLE 4.1   Chinese modern bank statistics from year 1896 to year 1937

year	# Bank			year	# Bank		
	founded	bankrupt	net surviving		founded	bankrupt	net surviving
1896	1	0	1	1924	7	5	55
1902	1	1	1	1926	7	7	57
1906	2	2	1	1928	16	5	69
1908	4	3	5	1930	18	6	89
1910	1	0	6	1932	13	4	108
1912	14	10	11	1933	15	3	120
1914	3	1	14	1934	22	4	138
1918	10	6	22	1935	18	0	156
1920	16	14	31	1936	5	0	161
1922	27	19	48	by Jun. 1937	3	0	164

Source: The department of economic research of China: Quanguo yinhang nianjian (The national yearbook of banks [1937]), A7 – A8, A24 – A25.

Figure 4.1 (Bank Statistics) further documents the development of the Chinese modern banks in the Republic period. Since the first domestic bank was established in year 1897, the scale of banking sector had not changed significantly until year 1911, the year when the Qing dynasty collapsed. There were two periods, in which the banking business flourished. The first was around 1920s with the total number of modern Chinese banks soaring from 22 in year 1918 to 55 in year 1924, yet with a high rate of bankruptcy.

Chapter 4 Connections and Performance: The Impact of Interlocking Directorates

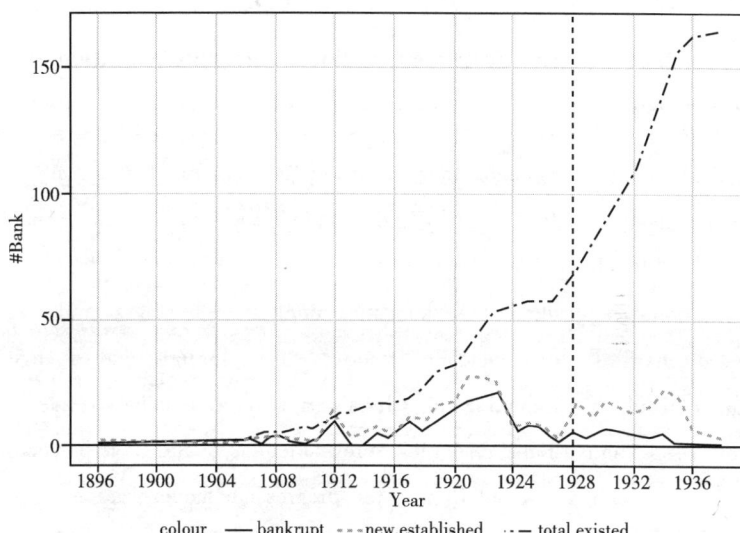

FIGURE 4.1 Bank statistics

Notes: The figure shows the total number of the Chinese modern banks in the Republic period. Blue, green, and red line indicates the total number of banks, newly established banks and banks went bankrupt, respectively. The two vertical dashed lines demonstrate the collapse of Qing Dynasty in 1911 and the beginning of Nanjing decade in 1928. Source: The department of economic research of China: Ouanguo yinhang nianjian (The national yearbook of banks [1937]), A7 - A8, A24 - A25.

One of the important features of the banking sector during this time period was the business cooperation among the major banks. For instance, The Shanghai Bankers' Association (SBA), a financial organization that helps promote the welfare and coordinate the banks' strategic plans, was established in year 1918, and by year 1931, its members had increased to 29 from the original 7. Leader of the major banks appear to have believed that only by cooperating their banks would survive the fierce competition and expand further. ①

4.2.2 Relation with the traditional financial institution and foreign banks

The Chinese financial market during the last few decades of the Qing dynasty was dominated by native financial institutions and foreign banks. "Piaohao" and "Qianzhuang", the main native financial institutions, controlled the domestic remittance business and the credit markets for domestic trade, while foreign banks had monopolized the financing of China's import and export trade②. However, "native bank resources were inadequate, and their personal manner of dealing did not fit into the progressive modernization", so that "they failed to keep pace with the changes of the country"③. Meanwhile, foreign banks lost the control of the ball in this match, since they were forced to give up some of their privileges in China in the course of the period. Tamagna (1942, P. 118) concludes that the position of the foreign banks by year 1937 was one of "necessary cooperation" with, rather than "control" of, the Chinese official financial policy.

By contrast, with expansions and concentration, modern Chinese banks held 81% of China's capital power by 1936 and become

---

① This saying is a summary of the leader's views of the major banks in China by author. Details see *Twenty years of history of Shanghai Commercial and Saving Bank*, 1936, 1sted..

② See Tamagna (1942) and Ji (2003) for a comprehensive introduction of Chinese financial system in the early 20th century.

③ Tamagna (1942, P. 80).

Chapter 4 Connections and Performance: The Impact of Interlocking Directorates

the dominant role in Nanjing decade (from year 1927 to year 1937). Table 2.2 goes into the details about the power balance among native financial institutions, foreign banks and the modern Chinese banks.

Given the historical context I described above, I choose the Nanjing decades (from year 1927 to year 1937) to conduct my analysis. The reasons are as follows. Firstly, traditional financial institutions (i.e Piaohao and Qianzhuang) and foreign banks had been un - ignored power in Chinese financial market. Together with Chinese modern banks, they are considered as "three king - doms" by some historians. As native banks and foreign banks become supporting roles in the 1930s as table 4.2 [Capital power in the Chinese financial market (1936)] illustrates, I am able to concentrate on the modern banking industry with less considering the side effects that native and foreign banks may bring into the analysis.

TABLE 4.2 Capital power in the Chinese financial market (1936)

Name/Items	Chinese Banks		Foreign Banks		Native Institutions		Total
	Amount	%	Amount	%	Amount	%	
Note	1946.7	87	284.7	13	0.0	0	2231
Deposits	4551.3	79	511.2	9	673.6	12	5736
Capital	402.7	67	113.7	19	84.2	14	600.6
Total	6900.7	81	909.6	11	757.8	9	8568

Note: Unit: C$1000000.
Source: Cheng (2003, P.78).

Next, Nanjing decade began with the end of warlord era and featured the establishment of the Nationalist government. In the year of 1937, China was united, and thanks to the relative stable political environment, modern Chinese Banks underwent their greatest expansion[①]. I avoided, by nature, some main factors that previous research suffered (e.g. precluding the impact of political turmoil and social turbulence), when I perform the empirical study.

Thirdly, recent research has been emphasizing the political connections of financial institutions in the Republic time period. Yet, in this paper, the judicious choosing of the time period prevents my results from interference of governmental linkage to a certain extent, as Cheng (2003, P. 92) highlights that albeit the government tired greatly to control the banking business, its efforts had a minimal impact upon the operation of Chinese banks until 1935.

In sum, aside from traditional financial institutions and foreign banks, modern Chinese banks were the absolute mainstream with respect to the domestic business and trade in the Nanjing decades, where political impact remained at the lowest level. The empirical study I perform below prevents the interference of factors (e.g. political turmoil, interplay with other financial institutions and social instability) to some extent by focusing on the Nanjing decades.

4.3 The Relationship Between Board – connectedness and Performance

This section investigates the relationship between board level

---

① Cheng (2003, P. 68).

connections and the economic performance of banks. I provide a comprehensive description of the dataset, showing the main details and characteristics used in the empirical analysis, and introduce an econometric model to examine potential correlations.

4.3.1 Data and variables

My study is based on a full sample of modern Chinese banks (so excluding traditional financial institutions and foreign banks) during the period of year 1933 to year 1936. I collect accounting data of banks and the names and positions of their board members from *The National Yearbook of Banks* (from year 1934 to year 1937), which was published by the department of economic research of the Bank of China as an annual statistical overview about the banking sector. Additional data on the board of directors of each bank has been collected from the prospectus of banks contained in the *The National Yearbook of Banks* (from year 1934 to year 1937), which is used to identify board composition and corporate governance structures of individual banks. The data I collect on each director includes name, the position she/he holds in the respective institution, the city, and bank branch, for which she/he works. Due to the structure of the traditional Chinese names, the data does not really suffer from duplicate names. But to avoid any doubts, I complement the information of individual directors with their mid-names, birthplaces, and ages collected from various biographies and other sources.

On average, my dataset consists of 157 banks, resulting in an unbalanced panel of 628 bankyear observations for the four-year period from year 1933 to year 1936[①]. The resulting data does cover all relevant Chinese modern banks which operated in China during the time period in question.

4.3.2 Empirical framework

I examine the relationship between bank board well-connectedness and financial performance with a regression setup. My estimating equation takes the form

$$Performance_{i,t} = \beta_0 + \beta_1 Board\_connectedness_{i,t} + Bank\_Characteristics_{i,t} + \varepsilon_{i,t} \quad (4.1)$$

where the subscripts i, t indicate individualbanks and time periods. Performance is a vector that measures the financial institution's profitability, $Board\_connectedness$ and $Bank\_Ckaracteristics$ stand for the connectedness measures and firm-level characteristics, respectively.

I use return on assets (ROA) and Profit per staff member as performance measures. ROA is measured as:

$$ROA = \frac{Profits}{Assets} \quad (4.2)$$

and Profit per capita is calculated as follows:

$$Profits p.c. = \frac{Profits}{\#staff} \quad (4.3)$$

where Profits = net profits of a bank; Assets = total assets and

---

[①] Our sample suffers from an issue of accounting data availability: Accounting entries are either missing or not given, particular for small and rural banks. Therefore, the number of banks in the summary statistics, e.g. Table 4.4 and Table 4.5, decrease dramatically in some case.

#staff = number of total staff of a bank. Detailed variable descriptions are given in appendix B.1. Using Return of Assets (ROA) as a performance measure is consistent with related studies such as Larcker, So, and Wang (2013) and Dass et al. (2014), which is the main reason why ROA is superior to ROE. In addition, I utilize a relative variable, i.e. profit per staff member, to complement the focus on financial size with a measure on operational size. Both dependent variables are specified as the natural logarithm of these measures to reduce skewness.

The main independent variables in my models are board variables measuring the board well - connectedness and firm characteristic controls. Additionally, I control for year and bank fixed effects in these regressions. The measures for board connectedness and bank characteristics are further discussed in the following subsections.

4.3.3 Board connectedness measures: a network approach

The focus in the empirical analysis on the impact of board connectedness on bank performance and profitability builds on social network analysis (SNA). Analytic tools from social network theory are applied to annual interbank networks from year 1933 to year 1936 based on interlocking directorates between banks. The social network[①] consist of nodes, individual banks, and links, interlocking directorates between two banks, so banks form and adjust the network by allowing or ending the presence of directors on multiple bank

---

① For a typical network construction and description, see Jackson, Rogers, and Zenou (2016).

boards. A vast literature emphasis the potential benefits of being well-connected in a social network even in the general case. Among them, Jackson (2005) suggests that well-connected individuals may be better positioned for information access because links serve as a conduit for diffusion and El-Khatib, Fogel, and Jandik (2015) highlight their advantages in bargaining and negotiation, because the high position in the network provides more opportunities and reduces constraints.

Follow the pioneering ideas of Padgett and Ansell (1993), I use four central SNA measures to describe well-connectedness or network centrality of the individual bank in the social network: Degree, Closeness, Betweenness, and Eigenvector centrality [Larcker, So, and Wang (2013) and El-Khatib, Fogel, and Jandik (2015)]. Degree measures how many links an actor has with others in the network. Closeness keeps track of the ease of reaching other actors throughout the whole network. Betweenness describes the importance of an actor as an intermediary between other actors in the network. And eigenvector centrality is an indicator for the importance of an actor's direct connections through looking at the pattern of links of those connections. Appendix B.2 provides a brief introduction of these network measures and examples to illustrate the calculations.

These measures are derived for a set of inter-bank networks. Table 4.3 (Summary statistics of bank network characteristics) reports annual summary statistics for these networks. On average, I identify 157 unique banks across example years, among which I see an 13.2% increase in the number of banks from 144 to 163. Additionally, isolated vertexes, which are banks do not share any board members with other banks in the dataset, increased from 41 to 58 simultaneously as well. The fact partly reflects that shared directorates are not formed at random, and are more likely to be an outcome of strategic decisions① within certain parts of the sector. The last row of panel A presents the proportion of isolated banks in the whole network setting each year. Although the number of non – connected banks did increase significantly during the sample years, the set of connected banks remained a substantial majority of the whole sector.

To further characterize the structure of the interbanking networks, I tabulate the network characteristics of the largest component only (i. e. the biggest sub – network in which all nodes/banks are connected②). The average path length is the mean of the shortest number of steps separating any two actors in the component. The values span from 2. 4 to 2. 9, which indicate there are around 3 steps of separation between any two banks in the central component of the banking network. The value is far smaller than the "six degree of separation" widely documented in a number of different literatures [e. g. Gurevitch (1961), Travers and Milgram (1969) and Bakhshandeh et al. 2011], which again supports the "intentional formulation of interbanking ties" point of view mentioned above. The diameter of the central component is the longest degree of separation between any two firms. I observe an average diameter of 8, exhibiting features of "small worlds" s (Travers and Milgram 1967). The clustering coefficient is 0. 418, denoting that 42. 8% of the time two

---

① My finding is in line with Larcker, So, and Wang (2013), which studies the boardroom centrality in the US.

② That is, any banks in the sub – network can reach any other vertex in the component through board links.

banks connected with another particular bank are also linked with each other. These additional measures further reinforce the impression that interbank networks were not random but developed with a purpose. Consequently, I examine whether the pattern of network connections was related to financial performance, the most obvious purpose of strategic firm decisions.

TABLE 4.3 Summary statistics of bank network characteristics

Panel A: Descriptive Statistics bank network				
	1933	1934	1935	1936
#Banks	142	159	164	163
#Links	329	458	424	416
#Isolated Banks	41	45	54	58
Network density	0.033	0.036	0.033	0.032
Panel B: Summary statistics of central component				
#Banks	88	89	102	94
Avg. path length	3.026	2.512	3.396	2.903
Diameter	9	8	12	9
Clustering coeff.	0.41	0.40	0.41	0.41

Note: Panel A demonstrates annual summary statistics of aggregate bank Network from 1933 to 1936. A component in network is a subset of the network that all its vertexes are inter-connected. Isolated banks are those nodes, which have no connections to other vertexes in the network. Density is the proportion of observed ties (also called edges, arcs, or relations) in a network to the maximum number of possible ties. Thus, density is a ratio that can range from 0 to 1. The closer to 1 the density is, the more interconnected is the network. Panel B contains statistics summary for the primary component of our bank network. Average path length indicates the average shortest number of steps among two arbitrary banks (nodes). Diameter is an indicator shows the longest number of steps between any two nodes in the network, and clustering coefficient describes an enumeration of the proportion of vertex triples that form triangles, i.e., all three nodes pairs are connected by edges.

To understand that potential relationship I utilize four centrality measures (i.e. degree, closeness, betweenness and eigenvector centrality), which are actor – specific measures, so are calculated for each bank seperetely rather than for the network as a whole. Table 4.4 (Summary statistics of bank network measures by year) illustrates the values of these network measures for the full sample of banks.

TABLE 4.4 Summary statistics of bank network measures by year

Panel A: Descriptive Statistics 1933

	N	Mean	S. D.	Min	P25th	P75th	Max
Degree	92	5.391	6.177	0	0	9	29
Closeness	92	0.026	0.010	0.011	0.011	0.033	0.034
Betweenness	92	0.011	0.017	0.000	0.000	0.016	0.098
Eigenvector	92	0.132	0.209	0.000	0.023	0.161	1.000

Panel B: Descriptive Statistics 1934

	N	Mean	S. D.	Min	P25th	P75th	Max
Degree	123	6.683	7.997	0	1	11	49
Closeness	123	0.022	0.008	0.008	0.009	0.027	0.027
Betweenness	123	0.007	0.015	0.000	0.000	0.008	0.125
Eigenvector	123	0.088	0.163	0.000	0.009	0.111	1.000

Panel C: Descriptive Statistics 1935

	N	Mean	S. D.	Min	P25th	P75th	Max
Degree	130	5.231	6.350	0	0	9	31
Closeness	130	0.016	0.006	0.008	0.008	0.020	0.020
Betweenness	130	0.006	0.012	0.000	0.000	0.010	0.087
Eigenvector	130	0.084	0.169	0.000	0.009	0.089	1.000

Panel D: Descriptive Statistics 1936

	N	Mean	S. D.	Min	P25th	P75th	Max
Degree	126	4.159	5.782	0	0	6	24
Closeness	126	0.012	0.004	0.008	0.008	0.016	0.016
Betweenness	126	0.003	0.008	0.000	0.000	0.003	0.046
Eigenvector	126	0.081	0.180	0.000	0.007	0.059	1.000

Notes: Panel A to D provides the number of banks and network measures for each year from 1933 to 1936. Network measures (Degree, Closeness, Betweenness, Eigenvector) are detailed in appendix B.2.

4.3.4 Bank characteristics

Based on similar research [e.g. Deloof and Vermoesen (2016), Acheson et al. (2016b), Nguyen, Hagendorff, and Eshraghi (2015)], I include as controls a set of characteristics and potential determinants for the financial performance of each bank: firm size, age, board size, number of cities in which a bank has branch, total staff number, liquidity [(reserve fund + cash on hand)/total deposits], leverage (total deposits/total assets), and investment volume in securities (the sum of investment in securities of a bank, including stocks, real estate and government bonds).

I control for bank size by including the natural logarithm of total assets (*Size*) and the total number of employees (*# staff*). Similarly, the number of cities (*# city*), in which banks carry on their business, is also included to test for a systematic difference due to geographic scale of operations. I use the number of years in operation as measured by the number of years since establishment, to track the maturity of the firm (*operation year*). A first operational variable included is the leverage ratio (*leverage*), while I capture the liquidity of a bank's assets by introducing a ratio (*Liquidity*) of how well a bank manages to match the maturity of its deposit with cash and financing instruments. Following Acheson et al. (2016b), I also include board size (*#board members*), which ranged from 1 to 39 with a mean of 12.7, to capture governance and control effects. Since the profitability of modern Chinese banks is likely dependent on speculation in government securities (Cheng 2003), I extract security investment information (*investment in securities*) from

Chapter 4 Connections and Performance: The Impact of Interlocking Directorates

balance sheets and include it. Furthermore, Larcker, So, and Wang (2013) suggests that the profitability of a firm is correlated with its prior performance, I therefore follow the idea by attaching the one-year-ahead profitability indicators to the regression (lag (ROA) and Lag ($Profit\ per\ capita$)).

Descriptive statistics of relevant bank characteristics are reported in Table 4.5 (Descriptive statistics of bank characteristics from year 1933 to year 1936). The banks in my sample tend to be young firms: they were on average only operational for 10 years with the highest value of 29 years for the Bank of China.

TABLE 4.5   Descriptive statistics of bank characteristics from year 1933 to year 1936

Statistic	N	Mean	St. Dev.	Min	Max
ROA	471	0.016	0.014	0.0002	0.108
net profit (in millions)	471	0.31	1.18	0	17.1
total assets (in millions)	471	42.13	155.15	0.0058	1803
#board members	470	12.736	4.701	1	39
#city	469	5.537	12.200	1	156
Age	360	10.211	7.423	1	29
#Staff	471	180.431	392.840	5	3505
liquidity	431	0.212	0.368	0.004	4.755
investment in securities (in millions)	413	4.28	16.28	0	252.1
leverage	470	0.642	0.467	0.032	7.160

Notes: This table provides a descriptive statistics of the bank main characteristics. The corresponding sample observations ($obs.$), mean, and standard deviation ($s.d.$), minimum and maximum of the values are reported. Refer to the main text for detail. Variable definitions are provided in appendix B.1.

4.3.5 Empirical Results

Columns 1 to 4 of table 4.6 (Bank performance regression) present the results from regressing ROA on the set of bank control variables and each of the four network measures. The t-values are shown in parentheses and are based on cluster robust standard errors. In the regression, I also include bank and time (two-way) fixed effects to account for both cross-sectional as well as time series dependence in the residuals. The results demonstrate that closeness centrality, as one measure of network connectedness, was significantly related to the firm's return on assets. The coefficient is 0.007 with a standard error of 0.003, showing that the improvement of closeness in network connection enhances the agent's annual ROA by 0.7%.

Columns 5 to 8 report the regression results when I use the other dependent variable, i.e. profit per staff member. The results are consistent with the outcomes for ROA. Again, closeness is the only measure that shows a statistically significant association with a bank's profitability. Given the robust correlation between the network measure and returns of a bank, the econometric results indicate that the interbank network had to positive impact on the operations of involved banks. However, the other three measures of network characteristics appear insignificant in both regressions, which indicate that they did not capture any relevant linkage between firms.

The empirical results raise the question whether Closeness, as a network centrality measure, is really substantially different from the

TABLE 4.6 Bank performance regression

	ROA				Dependent variable: Profit per capita			
	(1)	(2)	(3)	(4)	(5)	(6)	(7)	(8)
Degree	0.001 (0.001)				0.068 (0.114)			
Closeness		0.007* (0.003)				0.651** (0.321)		
betweenness			-0.007 (0.126)				0.648 (11.574)	
Eigenvector				0.003 (0.009)				0.526 (0.845)
Size	-0.005*** (0.002)	-0.005*** (0.002)	-0.005*** (0.002)	-0.005*** (0.002)	0.805*** (0.156)	0.786*** (0.154)	0.815*** (0.156)	0.820*** (0.155)
D/S ratio	-0.003 (0.003)	-0.002 (0.003)	-0.003 (0.003)	-0.003 (0.003)	0.533** (0.264)	0.566** (0.262)	0.538** (0.266)	0.522* (0.266)

Continued

		ROA				Dependent variable: Profit per capita			
	(1)	(2)	(3)	(4)	(5)	(6)	(7)	(8)
#Covered cities	-0.001 (0.001)	-0.001 (0.001)	-0.001 (0.001)	-0.001 (0.001)	-0.211** (0.090)	-0.214** (0.089)	-0.213** (0.091)	-0.204** (0.091)
Age	-0.004 (0.003)	-0.003 (0.003)	-0.003 (0.003)	-0.003 (0.003)	-0.303 (0.258)	-0.278 (0.251)	-0.273 (0.254)	-0.278 (0.253)
lag(ROA)	0.203*** (0.052)	0.211*** (0.052)	0.201*** (0.052)	0.202*** (0.052)				
lag(profit)					-0.182*** (0.063)	-0.167*** (0.063)	-0.183*** (0.063)	-0.184*** (0.063)
#staff	-0.0002 (0.004)	0.0001 (0.004)	-0.0001 (0.004)	-0.0004 (0.004)	0.796** (0.342)	0.829** (0.339)	0.800** (0.345)	0.770** (0.346)
Individual fix effect	Yes	Yes	Yes	Yes	Yes	Yes	Yes	Yes
Time fix effect	Yes	Yes	Yes	Yes	Yes	Yes	Yes	Yes

Continued

	ROA				Dependent variable: Profit per capita			
	(1)	(2)	(3)	(4)	(5)	(6)	(7)	(8)
Observations	334	334	334	334	334	334	334	334
R^2	0.130	0.143	0.129	0.130	0.259	0.271	0.258	0.259
Adjusted R^2	0.087	0.095	0.086	0.086	0.172	0.180	0.171	0.172
F Statistic (df = 7; 222)	4.752***	5.300***	4.703***	4.720***	11.094***	11.817***	11.027***	11.100***

Note: Column 1 to 4 contains the results from regressing bank's return on assets (ROA) on network measures of bank centrality in the network with various control variables. ROA is the bank's net income scaled by the total asset. Descriptions of degree, closeness, betweenness, and eigenvector are detailed in the main text. Size refers to the natural logarithm of total assets of the individual bank in Chinese yuan. D/S ratio = $\frac{\#boardmembers}{\#staff}$. Lag (ROA) and Lag (Profit) show the corresponding measure of the previous year. # Staff and # Covered cities indicate the natural logarithm of the total number of employees and branch coverage of individual bank, respectively. Age is the natural logarithm of the number of years that bank had been in operation since the establishment. Column 5 to 8 shows the regression results with Profit as dependent variable. Profit shows the natural logarithm of net income after working expense not included in the calculation of gross profit have been paid in Chinese yuan. Year and individual fixed effects are included. Robust standard error are reported in parentheses. The symbols ***, **, and * denote significance at the 1%, 5%, and 10% levels, respectively.

other three measures, as it seems to the only to capture a relationship between the network structure and bank performance. To explore the variation between the four network measures, Table 4.7 (Principle components analysis of network measures) reports a principal component analysis (PCA) of these four centrality measures. The first and second components[1] capture together 85.5% of the variation in Degree, Closeness, Betweenness, and Eigenvector. Using the information of both components, I reframe the original network measures along new dimensions of components to demonstrate the underlying structure in the data. Figure 4.2 (A variable map of the principle component analysis) highlights the resulting factor map of the network measures. While Degree, Betweenness, and Eigenvector measure the network centrality along dimension 1, Closeness is significantly differed from other indicators, explaining more variation along dimension 2. The results clearly suggest that Closeness carried substantially different centrality information in comparison to the other measures, and that centrality position seems to reflect a financially relevant network structure in the Chinese context in contrast to the other network indicators.

In sum, the econometric outcomes suggest that Closeness, as a measurement representing how easily a bank linked through interlocking directors to other boards across the sector, contribute positively to the financial performance of a bank. In other words, it is not just information from a small set of partners that improve a bank's

---

[1] The first component is with an eigenvector greater than one. I can interpret the first component as an aggregate measure capturing the overall well-connectedness of a bank.

profitability, but the ability to receive information and exchange resources throughout larger parts of the sector.

TABLE 4.7 Principle components analysis of network measures

	Importance of components:			
	Comp. 1	Comp. 2	Comp. 3	Comp. 4
Standard deviation	1.644	0.849	0.679	0.340
Proportion of Variance	0.675	0.180	0.115	0.028
Cumulative Proportion	0.6753	0.855	0.971	1.000

Notes: This table shows the summary information of the principle components analysis of network measures. Refer to the main text for details.

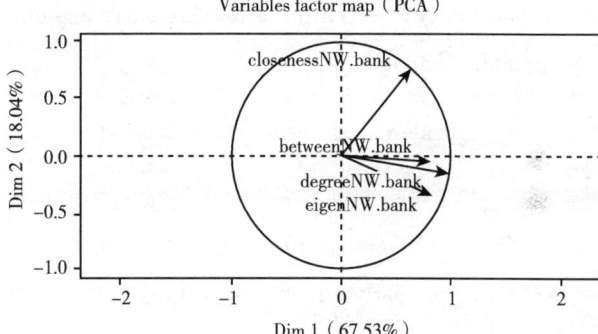

FIGURE 4.2 A variable map of the principal component analysis

4.4 Robustness and Further Tests

In this section, I provide further tests and explorations to find indication and evidence that are consistent with the main results above.

First, I highlight the prevalence and importance of interlocking directors in the modern banking sector by carrying out a "difference - in - mean" analysis, statistically comparing bank characteristics between banks with board links and banks without social ties. Then, I define an indicator, *board busyness*, to measure the extent to which an individual board connected with other financial institutions. Using this alternative measure of board links, I revisit the relationship between board links and banks' economic performance. Additionally, I provide a network neighborhood analysis to investigate the linking patterns among Chinese modern institutions and the channels through which social links contributed to the overall performance. Finally, I provide some explorations to address the potential endogeneity issue.

4.4.1 The prevalence of connected directors

In this paper, I define a director as connected (or busy) when one affiliates with more than one financial institution simultaneously (interlock director). Similarly, I consider a bank with (without) a busy director as connected (unconnected), and the corresponding board is likewise identified as a busy (non - busy) board[①].

Table 4.8 (Summary statistics of connected directors and banks) presents the annual summary statistics of director connections and the proportion of banks with connected directors. Overall, the

---

[①] I refer to abundant literature to define the connectedness of directors. Similar definitions are used by Larcker, So, and Wang (2013), Fich and Shivdasani (2006), Field, Lowry, and Mkrtchyan (2013) and El - Khatib, Fogel, and Jandik (2015).

number of connected directors remained stable between 123 and 150 across the time period with an exception in year 1934. Busy directors were spread over four fifth of the principal banks in my dataset, with 344 bankyear observations being connected and 127 unconnected. The data suggests that banks did have a strong proclivity to appoint connected individuals to their boards. It also reflects the ubiquity of interlocking directorates in the whole banking system, with each linked board having had 2 connected directors on average.

TABLE 4.8 Summary statistics of connected directors and banks

Year	# Director		# Banks		avg. # busy dirs/bank
	connected	unconnected	connected	unconnected	
1933	148	1267	101	41	1.04
1934	199	1429	114	45	1.25
1935	243	1459	108	54	1.5
1936	169	1530	104	58	1.04

Note: This table presents a summary statistic of the connected director and banks of the data. Directors are considered as connected if they affiliate with more than one bank. Column 2 – 3, and 4 – 5 report the number of banks with connected and unconnected director, separately. Avg. # busy dirs/bank refers to the the number of connected directors each bank on average. See text for the detailed data source.

To further explore the statistical correlation between "connectedness" and profitability of financial institutions, I begin with a difference – in – means test between banks with and without busy directors. Panel A of Table 4.9 (Difference in bank Characteristics between connected and unconnected banks) reports the comparison results of return on assets (ROA), return on equity (ROE) and profit per staff member, as profitability indicators, and variables describing firm characteristics. All variable definitions and descriptions are detailed in appendix B. 1. Profit per staff member for banks with at least one busy director was statistically and economically greater than that of banks without. However, the difference in ROA and ROE surprisingly remain negative. In other words, unconnected banks had a higher profitability as measured by ROA. One potential explanation for the result is that in the 1930s period, when investor protection was weak and firms were hit by economic uncertainty, business expansion to peripheral cities had a negative impact on banks' financial performance (Tong – na 2014). The difference of the number of the bank's operational cites between connected and unconnected banks, as captured by #City, is consistent with this point. I find linked banks covered three more cities on average than their unconnected counterparts. In other words, principle and connected banks operating in peripheral cities had lowered their economic performance while most unconnected banks were concentrated in the major metropolises where businesses were likely to deliver a higher profit margin. However, the result is not statistically significant after we control the banks characteristics using the propensity – score matching (PSM) approach. Overall, the comparison highlights that banks with connected directors were more profitable as measured by profit per staff member, bigger as seen by asset size, with more staff, and operated in more cities.

TABLE 4.9 Difference in bank Characteristics between connected and unconnected banks

Panel A: Statistic comparison

Variable	Bank-year obs. (unconnected)	Mean (unconnected)	Bank-year obs. (connected)	Mean (connected)	Mean diff connected - unconnected
Size	127	14.28	344	15.98	1.7 ***
Age	127	10.55	344	10.10	0.45
# City	127	3.15	344	6.41	3.26 ***
# Staff	127	74.01	344	219.72	145.71 ***
ROA	127	0.02	344	0.01	-0.006 ***
RoE	127	0.15	344	0.12	-0.021
Profit per capita	127	6.44	344	6.97	0.53 ***

Panel B: Propensity-Score Matching (PSM)

ROA	72	0.019	72	0.017	-0.003
ROE	72	0.15	72	0.12	-0.02
Profit per capita	72	6.62	72	6.99	0.3724 *

Note: The sample in Panel A consists Banks are categorized as connected if they have directors who affiliate with more than one bank. The board compositions and bank performance data are collected separately. For the bank board data, the sample covers 625 bank-years, with an average of 156 annual observations from 1933 to 1936 as Table 4.8. On the other hand, I have only collected the performance and firm characteristics data of 471 bank-year observations in total for the same time period.

As these correlations with ROA demonstrate, heterogeneity in bank characteristics poses a confounding problem for the simple comparison between banks in the two categories. To account for these effects of individual bank characteristics, I adopt a propensity-score matching (PSM) approach to select banks in the two categories. The matching is based on a set of bank characteristics, which are listed in Table 4.9①. Panel B of Table 4.9 shows the differences in average returns (again measured by ROA and profit per staff member) after applying the matching to adjust the set of included banks. My sample size becomes smaller, reducing to 72 observations for both groups. The gap in profits per staff members remains statistically significant with the same sign, again consistent with a positive impact of being connected on profitability. The difference in ROA and ROE, however, is now statistically insignificant between connected and unconnected banks after accounting for bank differences with the PSM approach. These two results indicate that the potential information and resource exchange through interlocking directorates might have had more of an impact on profitability through improving practical, operational efficiency of the banks than through their financial choices. The empirical outcome partly supports the point of view of Chapter 3 that interlocking directorates serves as a conduit for practical management knowledge and a defensive, insuring effect on strategic, financial choices.

4.4.2　Board composition and connectedness

The results of the SNA – based analysis above is consistent with the argument that busy directors and interlocking directorates facilitate an exchange of information or resources with positive consequences for these banks. The argument, however, only looks

---

① A specified analysis of the PSM and the matching results are detailed in appendix B.4.

Chapter 4 Connections and Performance: The Impact of Interlocking Directorates

at banks as closed entities, and does not take into account arrangements within a bank. A natural question now is whether the composition of a bank board, in particular the share of busy directors involved in an interlocking directorate, mattered for the performance of the bank? My expectation is that a higher proportion of busy directors on the board of a modern Chinese bank is beneficial for that bank. Consequently, I investigate that hypothesis with financial performance as outcome measure. More precisely, I capture the board busyness by using the number of directors, who were appointed to multiple boards, in relationship to the total number of board members. Formally:

$$Board\ busyness = \frac{\#Busy\ directors}{Board\ size} \quad (4.4)$$

The denominator is the total number of directors sitting on the board. The variable ranges from 0 to 1, with higher values indicating the extend to which a board reach an external board.

I estimate the model based on equation 4.1, introduced above, by replacing the network characteristic variable with the board busyness measure. As above, all of the panel regressions, control for bank fixed effects and year fixed effects, and standard errors are clustered at the bank level. The regression results are reported in Table 4.10 (Association between board busyness and bank performance).

Odd-numbered columns report prediction results, which control only for bank fixed effects and year fixed effects, and even-numbered columns include a large set of control variables. Column 1 and 3 report the baseline regressions without considering any characteristics of banks. Potentially, both outcomes suffer from an omitted variable issue. The coefficients of specifications (columns 2 and 4) are statistically significant and positive, suggesting board busyness is positively associated with bank performance. The estimated coefficients show that a bank with a 1% increase in board busyness increases the bank performance measured by ROA and Profit per capita by about 0.47% and 0.54%, respectively.

TABLE 4.10　Association between board busyness and bank performance

	Dependent variable:			
	ROA		Profit per capita	
	(1)	(2)	(3)	(4)
Board busyness	0.652 *** (0.237)	0.471 * (0.270)	0.153 (0.289)	0.542 * (0.291)
log (/ROA-1/)		-0.257 ** (0.116)		
log (/net_profit-1//staffNo)				-0.131 (0.124)
Size		-0.268 * (0.162)		0.391 *** (0.146)
log (no_of_board_members)		0.542 * (0.280)		0.615 ** (0.295)
Age		-0.141 *** (0.038)		-0.155 *** (0.039)
log (staffNo)		0.182 (0.203)		

Continued

	Dependent variable:			
	ROA		Profit per capita	
	(1)	(2)	(3)	(4)
log (liquidity)		0.082 (0.090)		0.069 (0.095)
leverage		−0.016 (0.087)		−0.047 (0.092)
log (investment_in_securities)		0.010 (0.047)		0.014 (0.049)
log (no_of_branch_covered_city)		−0.225** (0.089)		−0.278*** (0.093)
Bank fixed effect	Yes	Yes	Yes	Yes
Time fixed effect	Yes	Yes	Yes	Yes
Observations	470	319	470	319
R^2	0.018	0.161	0.001	0.139
F Statistic	5.573** (df=1; 306)	4.058*** (df=10; 211)	0.280 (df=1; 306)	3.808*** (df=9; 212)

Notes: * $p < 0.1$; ** $p < 0.05$; *** $p < 0.01$. All dependent and independent variables, excluding dummies, age, are logged. ROA and profit per capita, as independent variables are lagged one year. The OLS coefficients are reported, with the t‑statistics in parentheses.

The control variables have expected signs. Interestingly, the bank size (natural log of total assets) is positively related with profit per staff member but negatively with ROA, reflecting that marginal return on capital was declining in the banking sector in the 1930s, yet larger banks were still able to maintain greater profitability in average net income per staff. Some bank characteristic variables are not statistically significant (e. g. liquidity, leverage and securities investment), presumably because they did not vary enough over the time span and thus their impacts were captured by bank fixed effects. In addition, the significant outcome of bank age shows that equity returns tend to decline over a bank's lifetime, elucidating that banks become less dynamic as they age.

In summary, the evidence supports the hypothesis that the higher the share of board members of a modern Chinese bank that were involved in an interlocking directorate, the better the performance of that bank. In connection with the results above, including the absence of a direct effect of the degree measure as well as the differentiation between ROA and profit per staff member for the basic board connections, this points towards interlocking directorates as a conduit to improve the practical management know-how of board members. The exposure to multiple boards and the increase in the number of fellow bank directors point seemingly improved the management capabilities of involved bankers. While Chapter 3 demonstrates that a bank's financial choices are influenced through interlocking directorates, the indication of the results here suggest that practical management and operational efficiency also profited through banker's involvement in an interlocking directorate.

4.4.3 Network neighborhood analysis

Colvin, Jong, and Fliers (2015) suggests that interlocking directorates measure the relative independence of a bank, since banks with more interlocking directors are potentially more powerful in terms of financial and industrial dominance. Therefore, a bank's network neighbors, the other banks with which a bank is connected, may contribute to the overall performance, and further impact the bank's profitability. Based on this idea, I posit the hypothesis that a bank residing higher in the 'hierarchy' (i.e. positioning more central and thus having higher profitability) did possess more connections to well-performing banks.

I test this by comparing a summary measure of banks' network neighborhood, neighborhood quality, based on the rank of banks' centrality. To capture neighborhood quality, I use the same measures as Colvin, Jong, and Fliers (2015). Specifically, I measure the average values cross interlocks of asset size, leverage, ROA, and liquidity of all neighborhood banks, to which an individual financial institution connects, to capture the characteristics of neighborhood banks. I also calculate a Herfindahl - Hirschman index (HHI) to measure the level of concentration of a bank's neighborhood. In particular, I measure asset size concentration with the equation

$$HHI = \sum_{i=1}^{N} \left(\frac{s_i}{S}\right)^2 \quad (4.5)$$

where s_i/S indicates each interlock's total assets relative to the sum of total assets of all interlocked banks[1].

To rank banks' network centrality, I use Closeness and the principal component score (PCA) developed in section 4.3.5. Based on the empirical results in Table 4.6, Closeness is the most

---

[1] Assume, for instance, firm A shares board directors with firm B and firm C, both with a size of $1 million in assets. The HHI index will equal $(1/2)^2 + (1/2)^2$, so 0.5.

appropriate measure to capture relevant network centrality information while PCA catches the overall variation (nearly 70% of the overall variation as shown in Table 4.7) in the Degree, Closeness, Betweenness, and Eigenvector centrality measures.

Panel A of Table 4.11 (The comparison of network neighbor characteristics based on centrality) classifies banks into quintiles based on Closeness. Quintile 1 represents those banks that are the least connected in the network I constructed in section 4.3.3, while quintile 5 stands for those banks with the highest Closeness score. Except for the average neighbor bank's liquidity, I, indeed, find a significant difference of neighborhood characteristics between most and least central banks. On average, most-connected banks had network neighbors with a lower ROA[①], but higher liquidity and more concentrated assets structure. In panel B of Table 4.11, I use an alternative centrality measure, namely PCA, to calculate the quintile in the comparison. A minor difference to the panel A is that, due to the nature of PCA, firms that fall in quintile 5 (least connected banks) are mostly those without interlocking directors and thus without neighbours in the network. I therefore compare the means between quintile 1 and 4. The outcome is unsurprisingly consistent with the result in panel A. For the least connected banks, their network neighbors did possess less assets, had a lower leverage but a higher ROA and average liquidity.

---

① The lower ROA reflects the decreasing marginal income of capital, since the well-connected firms in general associates with greater equipped capital. The finding is in line with the empirical analysis shown in table 4.6 and table 4.10.

TABLE 4.11 The comparison of network neighbor characteristics based on centrality

Panel A: Means for neigbourhood quintiles, based on Closeness centrality

Quintile by Closeness	Neighbor avg. assets	Neighbor avg. ROA	Neighbor avg. leverage	Neighbor avg. liquidity	Neighbor avg. HHI
Quintile 1 (least connected)	6925188.833	0.024	0.540	0.148	0.062
Quintile 2	56875911.554	0.017	0.546	0.395	0.319
Quintile 3	169604518.875	0.011	0.642	0.160	0.509
Quintile 4	130217977.884	0.012	0.683	0.152	0.587
Quintile 5 (most connected)	123982030.498 ***	0.013 ***	0.709 *	0.123	0.452 ***

Panel B: Means for neighborhood quintiles, based on PCA

Quintile by PCA	Neighbor avg. assets	Neighbor avg. ROA	Neighbor avg. leverage	Neighbor avg. liquidity	Neighbor avg. HHI
Quintile 1 (most connected)	142555776.682	0.011	0.711	0.146	0.359
Quintile 2	160909891.107	0.012	0.682	0.129	0.520
Quintile 3	123465523.131	0.012	0.639	0.163	0.674
Quintile 4	42108724.909 ***	0.018 ***	0.547 ***	0.359 *	0.355
Quintile 5 (least connected)	0.000	0.000	0.000	0.000	0.000

Note: The table presents descriptive statistics of means on the main characteristics of the bank's network neighbours from year 1933 to year 1936. Columns 2 to 6 measure the average cross interlocks of asset size, leverage, ROA, and liquidity of all neighborhood banks, to which an individual financial institution related, and the HHI. In panel A, banks are sorted into quintiles based on the Closeness while they are sorted into PCA. The symbols ***, **, and * denote significant difference in means of Quintile 1 and Quintile 5 (In panel B, Quintile 1 and Quintile 4) at the 1%, 5%, and 10% levels, respectively.

To summary, most - connected banks tend to be on average more connected with banks who have larger assets. However, due to the increased firm size, the return on assets has faded reflecting the decreasing marginal return to capital in the banking sector. On the other hand, neighborhood banks are more likely to have had on average a higher leverage and lower liquidity. Contrary to modern settings, this suggests that banks are more confident to face uncertainty and to deal with risk.

4.4.4 Additional analysis of endogenous concern

One potentially significant problem for my empirical study is the question of reverse causality. There could be plausible alternative explanations of the positive relationship between network connectedness and firm's performance. Further, the measures I introduce above in the empirical study could be correlated with unobserved or omitted bank characteristics that were correlated with economic performances. For instance, if busy directors, who had social connections and management expertise, were more likely to accept offers to join a board from well - performing banks, my results may reflect predominantly the matching between high - quality managers and banks rather than an effect of interlocking directorates.

I conduct a basic test to explore the potential endogeneity issues for my context. Specifically, in order to keep the change in board centrality exogenous, I restrict the sample of banks to those whose board composition remained unchanged from last period to the current period and examine the correlation between the banks's centrality and its future economic performance (1 - year - ahead). The implies that

Chapter 4 Connections and Performance: The Impact of Interlocking Directorates

any change to the bank's centrality measures are independent of the dependent performance variables.

Table 4.12 presents the results of conducting that estimation. ΔBetweenness, ΔCloseness, and ΔEigenvector refer to the change ratio of respective network measure from previous year to current year. Profit1 and ROA1 indicate the bank's future one-year-ahead profitability. Except the measure of Degree, I document a positive and statistically significant (at the 1% level of ΔBetweenness, ΔCloseness, and at 10% level of ΔEigenvector) association between changes in the network measures and future bank profitability. The outcome provides some indication that this alternative explanation, busy directors preferred to sit on the board of well-performing banks, is not as consistent with the observed developments. However, the restriction of the sample leads to drop in observations from 334 to 71, which might potentially because of some concern.

TABLE 4.12 Change of well-connectedness and future performance

	\multicolumn{6}{c}{Dependent variable:}					
	Profit1 (1)	ROA1 (2)	Profit1 (3)	ROA1 (4)	Profit1 (5)	ROA1 (6)
ΔBetweenness	0.433 *** (0.146)	0.438 *** (0.126)				
ΔCloseness			0.948 *** (0.284)	-0.157 (0.137)		
ΔEigenvector					-0.042 (0.073)	0.098 * (0.055)

Continued

	Dependent variable:					
	Profit1 (1)	ROA1 (2)	Profit1 (3)	ROA1 (4)	Profit1 (5)	ROA1 (6)
Constant	11.778 *** (0.212)	-4.370 *** (0.126)	12.279 *** (0.438)	-4.682 *** (0.213)	10.708 *** (0.200)	-4.517 *** (0.100)
Observations	71	71	138	138	125	125
R^2	0.566	0.398	0.401	0.315	0.104	0.188
Adjusted R^2	0.560	0.389	0.396	0.310	0.097	0.181
F Statistic	89.577 ***	40.192 ***	90.199 ***	60.248 ***	-1.120	27.855 ***

Note: ΔBetweenness, ΔCloseness, and ΔEigenvector refer to the change ratio of respective network measure from previous year to current year. Profit1 and ROA1 indicate the bank's future one-year-ahead profitability. Year and individual fixed effects are included. Robust standard error are reported in parentheses. The symbols ***, **, and * denote significance at the 1%, 5%, and 10% levels, respectively.

4.5 Conclusion

This study shows that modern Chinese banks were not isolated islands within the sector during the Nanjing decade. Board interlocks were prevalent among these financial institutions, which leaded to the conjection that this network provided an invisible channel for exchanging resources, information and management know-who. As these direct flows are unobservable, this paper offers SNA-based analysis to trace, explore and examine the implications of these inter-banking connections. The empirical outcomes highlight a high positive correlation between banks' profitability and its board connections throughout the sector.

The study also confirms the recent literature on interlocking directorates, by offering the evidence that inter – firms social connections play an essential role in the daily operation, particular in the environment where firms are facing instability both politically and economically.

However, this paper also points to more unexplored aspects, in particular corporate governance and the acquisition of management skills, of pre – communist Chinese banking. My hope is that this paper inspires future work to better understand the underlying economics driving the strong inter – dependencies among interlocking networks. Furthermore, the study partly explains the rapid development of Chinese financial institution in the 1930s. I hope that my findings contribute to point the direction of modern Chinese banking research towards models beyond the traditional historical paradigm, both theoretical and empirical, and demonstrate the usefulness of the social – network – based approach.

The Evolution of the Interlocking Directorate Network

The domestic Chinese banking sector flourished during the Republican Era, especially in the Nanjing Government period of the 1930s. The unstable environment, however, led banks in this sector to cooperate strongly with each other, building a dense web of interlocking directorates between them. While the literature has addressed the impact of interlocking directorates on firm performance, not much attention has been paid on the evolution of such networks of connections in general. I investigate the development of the interlocking directorate network between domestic Chinese banks from year 1933 to year 1936 to understand how financial institutions structure cooperation within the sector in response to unstable external environments and weak property rights. This paper uses a dynamic network simulation approach to address the inflection problem between bank performance and network formation, illuminating what factors underlay the network evolution and shaped the structure of cooperation between Chinese banks.

5.1 Introduction

Chinese banks patterned on Western example saw a dramatic rise during the interwar Republican era (Kong and Ploeckl 2018c). As this growth happened during a period of instability the sector reacted through a strong level of cooperation in the sector, which is seen institutionally through strong linkages of bank personal that goes far beyond simple clique relationships (Sheehan 2005). This paper investigates the business logic underlying the pattern of institutional ties between these Chinese banks during the last years of the Nanjing decade, the height of Chinese economic prosperity in the interwar period.

There is a large literature that focuses on the impact of institutional ties between companies on their economic performance. Such most relevant ties are interlocking directorates, the practice of directors or other executives exercising important roles in multiple companies at the same time. Such interlocking directorates have been shown to influence firms performance. This has been demonstrated in a wide range of settings from modern firms (Larcker, So, and Wang 2013) to Victorian stock companies (Braggion and Moore 2011), Dutch Banks (Colvin, Jong, and Fliers 2015), British interwar steel companies (Holmes and Ploeckl 2014) to the nascent domestic banking sector of China's republican era (Kong and Ploeckl 2018b). These studies however focus predominantly on the impact of these interlocks, financial and otherwise, but largely shy away from analysing the pattern and dynamics of the utilized networks between firms. This study fills this gap by quantitatively analysing the main drivers behind the evolution of the interlocking network between domestic Chinese banks during year 1933 to year 1936, the height of the Chinese Republican era.

The domestic banking sector arose with the end of the Imperial era and flourished throughout the Republican era until the Japanese invasion. By the mid 1930s more than 150 banks were active, eclipsing foreign banks as well as the traditional financial sector by controlling about 80% of bank capital in China. These banks formed an interest association, the Shanghai Bankers Association. One of its activities was the publication of an annual yearbook, which for a number of years contains extensive statistical information about these domestic Chinese banks. In particular for the years 1933 to 1936 a wide range of financial performance indicators, such as total assets, profits, and liquidity are available besides more general information like headquarter location, the number of cities served, the main focus of activities (real estate, etc) and the names of directors and executives. The latter allows the identification of directors in the employ of two or more banks, which I use to create a network of interlocking directorates between these banks.

Mizruchi (1996) categories potential reasons for such a tie between firms as collusion, cooptation and monitoring, legitimacy,

Chapter 5 The Evolution of the Interlocking Directorate Network

career advancement, and social cohesion. This paper focuses on the motives of the firm, rather than the individual director, therefore exploring in particular collusion and co – optation patterns between these banks.

The evolution of the network is analysed with a Stochastic Actor oriented Network model, the SIENA methodology. This method focuses on understanding the dynamic evolution of a network, where actors like banks, make decisions about ties with each other as well as other characteristics. The main intention is to illuminate the precise nature of inflection phenomena, so how networks and certain behaviour characteristics influence each other in their development. Practically, this approach specifies an objective function for each actor, consisting of a set of mechanisms. Each mechanism models a particular factor that potentially could affect the formation or dissolution of particular ties. The estimation then simulates the evolution of the model using this objective function and through comparison of the simulation outcomes with the actual observed network evolution data derives a parameter value for each mechanism, including statistical significance of these parameters. The exact nature of these mechanisms is fairly unconstrained, from the usual independent covariates of regular regression setups to characteristics of the existing network to interactions between multiple covariates and network structures.

A particular aspect of this situation is that the success of the sector happened within an environment with weak contract enforcement and property rights. This leads to the question of how the structure of the emerging banking sector developed. Weak contract enforcement could lead to a strong clustering and polarization effects with banks forming tight bonds to protect and insure each other within distinct groups, or ties could be widespread rather than clustered to facilitate more limited transactions over the whole sector rather than creating strongly competing groups of banks. This can be included through including mechanisms that reflect the effect of particular network structures, such as the tendency to form triplets or the impact of the number of existing ties on new ones.

Although the national government was not fully able to achieve strong institutions, including meaningful banking regulation, it nevertheless was involved in the banking sector through stakes and outright ownership of a number of important banks. As shown by Kong and Ploeckl (2018c), these public banks had a strong network of interlocking directorates with private institutions. I test whether the nature of certain institutions as public banks had a particular influence on the network development and contrast banks owned by the national government with municipal and provincial institutions. Further I test whether the potential role of national level public banks remained constant over the time or changed with the monetary reforms in year 1935.

Results show that there were network effects, with a tendency to form triads and a decentralization effect due to a negative effect of the existing number of ties. A number of operational effects mattered, including the types and ages of two potential partner banks. Similarly, financial characteristics mattered, in particular the relative ratio of two banks' assets, while size on its own did not have an effect. The involvement of national public banks mattered, with the pattern

Chapter 5 The Evolution of the Interlocking Directorate Network

showing a strong swing from positive to negative effect with the 1935 financial reforms. Finally, the bank's financial performance, its levels of ROE and ROE growth, mattered for its tendency to expand its interlocking directorate network.

An important issue for analyzing the impact of these interlocking directorates is the question of possible endogeneity between the network and the financial performance of the involved firms. This is explored through expanding the model with including the Return on Assets as a second dependent variable. This leads to modeling the co-evolution of networks (interlocking directorates) and behavior (financial performance) within the same estimation and the inclusion of explicit interaction effects as mechanisms driving the two outcomes. Results confirm the outcomes found in the network only estimation but do not clearly support a strong impact of interlocking directorates on the financial performance of the banks. The final section will discuss the inconsistency between them and the results of the preceding chapter. We believe that the effect is more likely obscured by the constraints of the estimation method rather than actually being absent.

5.2 Bank Network and Characteristics

The interlocking directorate network between modern domestic Chinese banks has been shown to link a large section of the whole sector tightly together (Kong and Ploeckl 2018c), to have a coordination effect with regard to policies (Kong 2018) as well as affect the profitability of these firms (Kong and Ploeckl 2018b). This study focuses on the evolution of that network and does so by utilizing the data presented of those three studies. Consequently, the following exposition of the utilized data is directly adapted from them as well.

The analysis of the network formation will regard banks as central actors rather than the involved individuals. This implies that there are two main data requirements, namely the interlocking directorate network between the banks and second, characteristics of the actors, so characteristics of the involved banks.

I look at the last years of the Nanjing decade, in particular from year 1933 to year 1936, which implies that the sector had been substantially established at that time, but was nevertheless still adjusting internal network structures over these years. This allows to illuminate the principles driving this network evolution by focusing on this time period.

5.2.1 Interlocking Directorate Network

As indicated above, this study focuses on modern Chinese banks from year 1933 to year 1936. This excludes traditional financial institutions as well as foreign banks. While a number of Chinese banks did interact with foreign financial institutions, the two banking sectors did remain clearly separated. This is similar to the clear distinction of these institutions from the traditional financial institutions. Besides, as I showed earlier in Table 5.2 modern-style Chinese banks had risen to dominance by the 1930s with collective bank capital surpassing that of foreign and traditional institutions combined. Consequently, I only look at domestic Chinese financial institutions that were patterned on western banking institutions.

Chapter 5　The Evolution of the Interlocking Directorate Network

The main data source is *The National Yearbook of Banks*, which was published by the department of economic research of the Bank of China. The annual issues for the years from 1934 to 1937 contain summaries about the whole sector as well as accounting and operational data about individual banks including names and positions of their directors and managers. I construct the dataset of boardroom composition by extracting information from the summary descriptions of the sector as well as the included annual reports of individual banks.

These data, which include names, positions, and branch locations, are used to identify interlocking directorates by matching names of listed directors of all included banks. Due to the structure of traditional Chinese names, duplicate names are not a significant concern. Nevertheless I address this by complementing the basic information about individual directors with information on middle name, birthplace, and age from various biographies and other sources[1].

For a very small number of institutions the recorded data are substantially incomplete or inconsistent. I exclude these as they are very small, local institutions and account for only a minuscule proportion of the full dataset. Consequently, my final sample consists of an unbalanced panel of 628 bank – year observations for the four – year period from year 1933 to year 1936[2]. While the coverage is complete for interlocking directorates, some of the operational and

---

[1]　The major data source is (Jiang 2014).

[2]　Specifically, the dataset includes board information of 142, 159, 164, and 163 banks from 1933 to 1936 respectively.

other bank characteristics are missing for a small number of observations.

Table 5.1 (Summary statistics of connected directors and banks) presents annual counts of directors and banks involved in interlocking directorates. Despite the unbalanced nature of the panel being responsible for a substantial share of the fluctuations, a consistent picture emerges that a comparatively small number of directors were linking together a major share of the whole domestic Chinese banking sector.

TABLE 5.1 Summary statistics of connected directors and banks

Year	# Director		# Banks		avg. # busy dirs/bank
	connected	unconnected	connected	unconnected	
1933	148	1267	101	41	1.04
1934	199	1429	114	45	1.25
1935	243	1459	108	54	1.5
1936	169	1530	104	58	1.04

Notes: This table presents a summary statistic of the connected director and banks of the data. Directors are considered as connected if they affiliate with more than one bank. Column 2 - 3, and 4 - 5 report the number of banks with connected and unconnected director, separately. Avg. # busy dirs/bank refers to the the number of connected directors each bank on average. See text for the detailed data source.

Furthermore, the average number of directors per bank involved in interlocking directorates is close to two, implying that many banks were linked in different directions rather than just by a single link. [1].

---

[1] This also indicates that interlocking directorates are not just representing direct ownership and control by a single owner, but point to at least multiple owners or other relationships between banks.

Chapter 5 The Evolution of the Interlocking Directorate Network

This is confirmed by Figure 5.1 (Bank network connection and assets cumulative distributions in 1933), which shows the number of links per bank in year 1933. Although there is a substantial number of banks that are completely unconnected and some with a single link only, the majority of banks form part of two or more interlocking directorates.

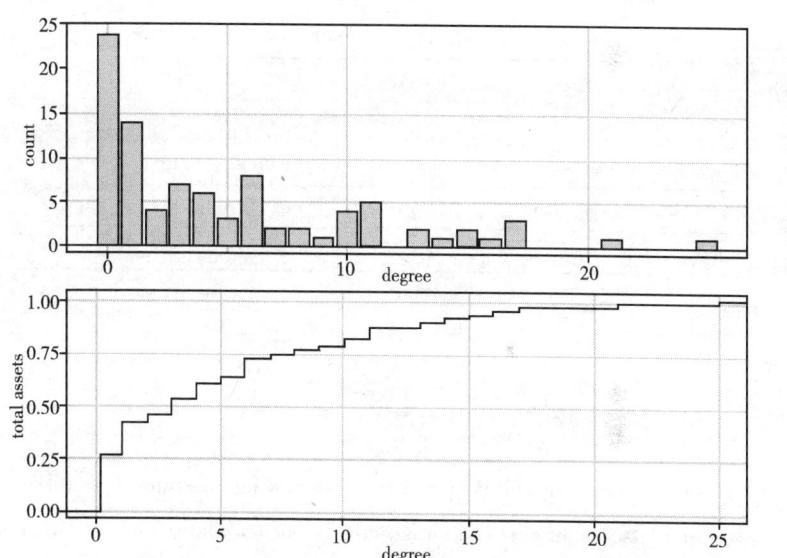

FIGURE 5.1 Bank network connection and assets cumulative distributions in 1933

As Table 5.1 indicates, the network of interlocking directorate was changing substantially over the four years. Although a certain amount is due to the unbalanced nature of the panel a good number of banks, according to Table 5.2 (Summary statistics of bank board composition change rate) about a quarter to a third, changed their board composition during the course of a year. As interlocking directorates are defined by board members, changes in board membership obviously has implications for the persistence and stability of the interlocking directorate network. Consequently, the network was clearly not a static, inert structure but was continually adjusted and modified by the involved banks.

TABLE 5.2 Summary statistics of bank board composition change rate

Bank Type	1933	1934	1935	1936
All	base year	0.273	0.293	0.325
Central banking group	base year	0.410	0.155	0.221
Local official banking group	base year	0.256	0.432	0.438
Ordinary banking group	base year	0.272	0.264	0.301

Note: This table provides the change rate of board directors over years with 1933 as the base year. Details refer to the main text.

5.2.2 Bank Characteristics

The source material for the interlocking directorates (ID) network also contains information about a number of bank characteristics as shown in Table 5.3 (Descriptive statistics of bank characteristics from year 1933 to year 1936).

TABLE 5.3 Descriptive statistics of bank characteristics from year 1933 to year 1936

Statistic	N	Mean	St. Dev.	Min	Max
ROA	471	0.016	0.014	0.0002	0.108
net profit (in millions)	471	0.31	1.18	0	17.1
total assets (in millions)	471	42.13	155.15	0.0058	1803

Chapter 5 The Evolution of the Interlocking Directorate Network

Continued

Statistic	N	Mean	St. Dev.	Min	Max
#board members	470	12.736	4.701	1	39
#city	469	5.537	12.200	1	156
Age	360	10.211	7.423	1	29
#Staff	471	180.431	392.840	5	3505
liquidity	431	0.212	0.368	0.004	4.755
investment in securities (in millions)	413	4.28	16.28	0	252.1
leverage	470	0.642	0.467	0.032	7.160

5.3 Mechanisms and Simulations

Each interlocking directorate is a binary dyad between two actors. There are a number of standard regression approaches, most notably logistic regressions, that can be used to analyze binary data with each dyad, so each pair of banks, as an observation. There are, however, two main concerns in doing so. First, there is a potential endogeneity between an interlocking directorate and other characteristics of the banks involved. And second, there is potential violation of the independence between observations through a form of spatial dependence, as the formation of an interlocking directorate might have depended on the existing network links between other banks.

The main reasons that these two issues are of concern are that they distort the results and are an obstacle for identifying a clean direction of causality. In response to this I choose to utilise an approach that analyses the dynamic adjustment of the network, including the particular shape of a reciprocal influence and the impact of the wider network structure. Instead of correcting for endogeneity and dependence, I essentially incorporate them as potential factors affecting the evolution of the network. To achieve this I use the SIENA methodology, which utilizes simulation methods to understand and identify factors driving the dynamic adjustment of network structures.

5.3.1 SIENA

The SIENA[①] method has been recently developed[②] in sociology, as illustrated by Steglich, and Pearson (2010) and Snijders, Bunt, and Steglich (2010), and is slowly adopted in political science (Manger and Pickup 2016) and economics (Esteves and Ploeckl 2016).

The main impetus for its development is to understand the dynamic evolution of actor oriented networks. This treats network ties as outcomes and assumes that agency to decide about ties rests with individual actors. Such actors can be individuals, who form for example friendship networks with other individuals (Block and Grund 2014; Cheadle et al. 2013), firms and the cooperative networks between them (Balland, De Vaan, and Boschma 2012; Withers, Kim, and Howard 2018), or countries that form agreements and alliances with each other (Manger and Pick up 2016; Esteves and

---

① SIENA stands for Simulation Investigation for Empirical Network Analysis.
② The practical implementation is done with a software package in R labelled RSiena.

Chapter 5 The Evolution of the Interlocking Directorate Network

Ploeckl 2016). Withers, Kim, and Howard (2018) resembles the setup in this paper as it looks at interlocking directorates between US firms, supporting the application of this methodology to historical Chinese banks.

In any of these setups the actors' decisions to change network ties potentially depend on the state of the network, other networks or potential actor characteristics. Such potential dependency incurs a number of problems for standard estimation methods as outlined later in this section. That traditional estimation methods focus predominantly on the identification of causal effects is not main concern of the SIENA approach. The focus is to better understand the actual mechanisms at work, so to better understand how the different influence factors and channels shape the decisions. The method also offers possibility to include individual actor behaviour, so specific actor characteristics rather than ties between actors, as outcome variables, but this carries substantial constraints and can only be in combination with a network as outcome variable.

The main idea is to detect the relevance of particular mechanisms and channels by simulating the evolution of the network, and potentially behaviour, and match the simulation outcomes against actually observed developments. This illuminates that factors improve that match and thereby are closely linked to the particular shape, path and evolution of networks and behaviours.

As the method is not really known in the economics or economics literature, this section focuses on introducing and explaining its practical structure. The exposition is therefore directly based on Esteves and Ploeckl (2016), which draws and builds upon the wider literature, in particular the fundamental works by by Steglich, and Pearson (2010) and Snijders, Bunt, and Steglich (2010).

The method differs in its focus from standard regression approaches in three central ways, first the potential endogeneity between two characteristics, second the standard assumption of independence between network tie outcomes and third the appropriateness of modelling events as a series of regular spaced, discrete steps.

The finance literature on interlocking directorate network effects, including Kong and Ploeckl (2018b), argues that the relationship between interlocking directorates and a positive impact on financial profitability usually runs from the network to the financial outcomes, rather than in the opposite direction. The evidence base for that claim, however, is limited and usual approaches to account for this, for example the use of Instrumental Variables, is not really feasible due to absence of suitable instruments.

Secondly, explaining the pattern of interlocking directorates, rather than their impact, implies the use of ties, pairs of actors, as outcome variables. Network theoretic approaches can explain the status of ties conditional on the status of ties between other actors, but if the outcome depends on status of other bank dyads, the independence assumption of the standard estimation approach is violated. There are some approaches to address this problem within standard econometric estimation approaches, for example Spatial Econometrics or Conley Standard errors. These approaches, however, have drawbacks, such as the required a priori specification of a spatial weight matrix, which makes them unsuitable here. In this

Chapter 5 The Evolution of the Interlocking Directorate Network

context the most obvious violation of the independence assumption is that individual directors are members of multiple boards, implying that multiple interlocking directorates between different bank pairs are directly related to each other as they are based on the same underlying person.

Another conceptual issue is the the discrete nature of the observations used in the analysis. Similar to most empirical analyses, many firm level approaches in economic history use annual or even less frequent data points. This not only turns underlying continuous processes into discrete steps, losing information in the process and creating the, likely strongly misleading, impression that all changes within one period happened at the same time. The order in which links between banks are created, or dissolved, within the same year, might potentially contain substantial and relevant information lost through this standardization. Also the volative environments imply that there might be more than one change happening over a year, with network links forming and dissolving fairly rapidly. Similarly estimation usually requires discrete steps of equal length, potentially complicating the estimation even further.

More practically, the following descriptions of the methodology cover the co – evolution of network and behaviour, however the network side of the description is fully applicable to a network only analysis. The basic starting point is to incorporate a wide range of mechanisms into the formation and development of the network structure to identify their respective effects onto tie formation and dissolution. This is expanded by incorporating behaviour changes to the set – up that adds a potential mutual dependence between ties and behaviour. To address this endogeneity problem, the approach shifts the conceptual model from a series of discrete choices to a continuous process whose state is observed at specific time points, with the recorded data taken as those observations. The network and the behaviour of involved actors are therefore taken as evolving continuously over the time period in question and their simultaneous modelling allows to account for mutual dependencies and multiple changes between the points of observations.

Structurally the modelling of mechanisms includes actor, dyadic and network structure covariates. The first are particular characteristics of the actors, for example the opening year or the number of branches of a bank, which are regular explanatory variables in a standard regression setup. Dyadic covariates are characteristics ofpairs ofactors. These can be direct tie variables, for example whether the headquarters of two banks are located in the same location or they are the same type of bank, or interacted actor variables, for example the ratio of the assets of the two banks. Furthermore, as pairs can be ordered, these dyadic variables can be directed and therefore asymmetric. Network structure covariates are variables stating the structural position of the actor within the network, for example the number of other banks a bank is linked to through an intermediary bank only.

Changes in the network as well as the behavioural status of individual actors are modelled as the outcome of a two-step process comprising two sub-processes, the first governs when the possibility to change the network or behaviour arises for an actor while the second then consequently determines whether an actual change will happen

Chapter 5 The Evolution of the Interlocking Directorate Network

once the opportunity is given. The first is governed by rate function while the second is determined by an evaluation function. The rate function is similar to a hazard rate function in a survival analysis set – up and determines the probability that the actor can make a change at any given point in time. Again similar to a hazard rate, this function can vary over time between countries and depend on covariates. Although they can be correlated due to this influence of covariates the rate functions for network changes and behavioural changes are independent of each other. Once the possibility of a change arises the evaluation function determines whether that change increases the utility of the actor and will consequently be implemented. As the rate functions are independent, the opportunity to change a behaviour will never arise at exactly the same time point as the opportunity to change the network. This implies that the evaluation function in each case does take the state of network respective the behavioural values as given. Once the opportunity arises the evaluation function is used to derive a value for each possible action, with these values consequently used to determine relative probabilities for each option to be taken.

Practically the set – up consists of a set of actors that are potentially linked to each other in a binary network. The analysis can focus exclusively on the development of the network ties between the actors. Adding actor characteristics allows to focus on the development of these behavioural values as well as the joint development of the network and the behavioural characteristics. Finally it is also possible to extend the system to add further networks or behaviour characteristics. The further discussion focuses on the joint evolution of network and behaviour as it combines the two archetypical cases and represents the commonly utilized explanatory system.

Returning to the formal description the rate functions, which determine the waiting times until the next change opportunities, are modelled by an exponential distribution with the following distribution function

$$g_i(t) = \lambda e^{-\lambda t}, \ t > 0 \qquad (5.1)$$

where $\lambda = \sum_i (\lambda_i^Z + \lambda_i^X)$ with λ_i^Z and λ_i^X as actor – and period – specific parameters for the behaviour rate respective network rate functions. This formulation implies that the probability that the next possible change actor i can make is a behavioural one is λ_i^Z/λ and for a tie change λ_i^X/λ.

Once an actor receives the opportunity to make a change, the respective evaluation function determines if and if so what change is maximizing the utility of the actor. Starting with the network structure the actor has three possible types of actions, initiate a new tie, dissolve an existing tie or retain the existing network without making a change. If there are n actors then this implies n possible actions consisting of changes in ($n-1$) ties to other actors as well as the retention of the existing structure. Formally the network evaluation function, which includes the mechanisms modelled by network structure, actor and dyadic covariates, is given by

$$f_i^X(\beta, \mathbf{x}, \mathbf{z}) = \sum_{k=1}^{m_1} \mathbf{fi}_k^X \mathbf{s}_{ik}^X(\mathbf{x}, \mathbf{z}) \qquad (5.2)$$

Following generalized linear statistical models, this function is assumed to be a linear combination of a set of *effects*, $s_{ik}(\mathbf{x}, \mathbf{z})$, which are functions defined on the state of the network and

Chapter 5 The Evolution of the Interlocking Directorate Network

behavioural variables. Particular examples will be discussed in a later section. Statistical parameters represent the importance of the respective effects so $f_i^x(\beta, \mathbf{x}, \mathbf{z})$ is the value of the evaluation function for actor i depending on the states x of the network and z of the behavioural variables. Additionally a random component is added to represent factors not modelled and general inherent randomness.

Similar to a multinomial logistic regression, this allows to calculate the probability of any single tie change shifting the network status from x to x'. Given the parameters of the evaluation functions this probability is:

$$P(x) = \frac{\exp[f_i^x(\beta, \mathbf{x}', \mathbf{z})]}{\sum_{x' \in C} \exp(f_i^x(\beta, \mathbf{x}', \mathbf{z}))} \quad (5.3)$$

This probability is for a directed network with a behavioural variable so tie x_{ij} can take the value 1 while x_{ji} is 0 (and vice versa). There are a number of possibilities to force the symmetry between x_{ij} and x_{ji} such that the network is undirected and ties are simple link between two actors. The options differ in their procedures about who proposes a change to a tie and whose consent is sufficient for creation or dissolution. One particular approach is 'unilateral initiative and reciprocal confirmation' where it is the decision by one actor (labelled as 'ego' in this case) to initiate a tie with another (labelled as 'alter) who then has to confirm the tie for it to be created. The probability that the tie is also in the interest of the alter is the following:

$$P(x) = \frac{\exp[f_i^x(\beta, \mathbf{x}', \mathbf{z})]}{\exp[f_i^x(\beta, \mathbf{x}, \mathbf{z})] + \exp[\mathbf{f}_i^x(\mathbf{fi}, \mathbf{x}', \mathbf{z})]} \quad (5.4)$$

This evaluation function only compares the value of the network with and without the potential change, it does not distinguish whether that change is a creation or dissolution of tie.

In case the potential change is to the behavioural value the actor has again the three types of choices, namely increase, decrease or retain the value. As the behavioural variable is required to be discrete, the potential increase or decrease is limited to exactly one step up or down. This restriction to a single step change is similar to the restriction to a single tie change in the case of the network structure. Furthermore, the network evaluation function is also equivalent in its components to its network counterpart:

$$f_i^z(\beta, \mathbf{x}, \mathbf{z}) = \sum_{k=1}^{m_2} fi_k^Z s_{ik}^Z(\mathbf{x}, \mathbf{z}) \qquad (5.5)$$

It is possible that the included effects s_{ik}^z are the same as those in the network evaluation function, and therefore that the same covariates drive the change in network ties and behaviour values. This is clearly not a reasonable assumption so correspondingly the sets of included effects will normally differ between the evaluation functions. Although the included effects differ, the probability for a particular change is formulated in the same way:

$$P(z) = \frac{\exp[f_i^z(\beta, \mathbf{x}, \mathbf{z}')]}{\sum_{z' \in C} \exp[f_i^Z(\beta, \mathbf{x}, \mathbf{z}')]} \qquad (5.6)$$

These functions are used in the simulation algorithm to execute the estimation. The idea is to sample parameter values with the goal of matching the characteristics of the simulated networks with those of the actual observed network. The estimation utilizes a Method of Moments approach, although alternatively a Maximum Likelihood as well as Bayesian approach are feasible as well. The algorithm results in an estimate for each parameter value and associated standard error as well as a t - statistic for its convergence. The latter provides a check whether the simulated values converged sufficiently close to the observed network values.

The sign of the parameter values and the standard error indicate the direction of the effect of the associated mechanism as well as the statistical significance of that effect. The estimated parameters for each effect should be interpreted as log - odds ratio. The explanatory covariate variables are centred on their mean, so if they are held at this rate the parameter values allow the calculation of an one - unit change in the mechanisms on the probability of an increase (or decrease) in the network (i.e. the number of ties) or the behavioural value.

This setup requires a number of assumptions to hold so that it is possible to interpret the results causally, especially with regard to influence and selection, i. e. endogeneity. Manger and Pickup (2016) summarizes them in the following:

- The observed network and behaviours are the outcomes of an underlying markov process in continuous time.
- The actors act conditionally independent of each other at any point in time conditional on the observed network, behaviour and covariates, therefore no simultaneous changes in the network[1] or behaviour by two or more actors exist.
- The changes in the network are conditionally independent of

---

[1] The requirement of reciprocal agreement to form a tie does not violate this assumption.

the changes in behaviour, in other words there cannot be simultaneous changes in network ties and actor behaviour.

- At any given time only one single tie can be changed and similarly behaviour can only be increased or decreased by one unit.

The particular nature of the research questions in this paper fits extremely well within the structure of SIENA methodology.

5.3.2 Mechanisms and Influence factors

The mechanisms in the evaluation functions represent the factors whose influence on the evolution of the ID network is tested, similar to the role of independent observations in a regression. To understand the evolution of the network, I include a number of factors categorized into network variables, operational characteristics, government links, financial characteristics, and financial profitability. Some of these mechanisms are also included in the behavioural extension, which looks at the development of profitability as an additional outcome.

Network variables reflect the influence of the existing network structure on its evolution. Practically I use the following mechanisms:

- *Degree*: this measures the number of interlocking directorates a bank already has.
- *Transitive Triads*: this indicates whether a particular link closes a link triad with a third bank.
- *Number of actors at distance* 2: this counts the number of banks the bank is linked to only indirectly through a third bank.
- *Degree of alter*: the number of interlocking directorates of the potential link partner.
- *Assortativity*: this tests whether the relative distribution of all

Chapter 5 The Evolution of the Interlocking Directorate Network

their IDs between the two potential partners matters.

Operational Characteristics contain variables that characterize practical, operational (rather than financial) aspects of a bank's business. The mechanisms are specified so that it is the characteristic of the 'alter' that is included, so practical it is in the first instance not the characteristic of the bank that initiates the link but that of any potential partner. The type of mechanism varies, some are derived for the characteristics of one bank only while others use those of both banks involved in a potential interlocking directorate.

- *Co – Location*: this binary variable tests whether banks with headquarters in the same location are more likely to link up.

- *Same Bank Type*: this binary variable tests whether banks are more likely to form links with banks of the same type.

- *Bank Opening*: this variable contains the year the bank was established, consequently testing whether its age matters.

- *Bank Opening difference*: this test whether the difference in age between two banks matters.

- *Branches*: this variable contains the number of locations where the potential partner bank maintained at least one branch.

- *Staff*: this variable measures the total number of staff the potential link partner employs.

- *Execs*: this tests whether the number of executives a potential partner has matters for the likelihood of a link.

- *Assets per Executive*: this variable contains the size of the assets per executive the potential partner bank had. This gives an indication of the extent of the responsibilities and experience of executives available for a potential link.

Government links are looking at the linkage between private and public banks.

- *Central Link*: this variable indicates if a pair of banks contains one of the banks from the Central banking group. This variable is also interacted with time dummies to test whether its effect changed systematically over the included years.
- *Local Link*: this variable indicates if a pair of banks contains one of the banks categorized as Province and city banks. This is used to contrast the reach of the national government with the engagement with local public banks.

Financial Characteristics contain mechanisms that build upon financial aspects of banks' operations and their strategic choices in that regard.

- *Asset ratio*: this is the ratio of two banks assets with the smaller divided by the larger (so 0.5 indicates one bank is twice the other, while 1 indicates equal size).
- *log Assets*: these is the logarithmic value of a potential partner bank's assets.
- *Leverage*: this measures how leveraged a potential partner is, calculated as (deposits all kind)/total assets.
- *Liquidity*: this measures how liquid a potential partner is, calculated as (reserve fund + cash on hand)/deposits all kind.
- *Bonds/Deposits*: this measures the ratio of a potential partner bank's investment in securities, notably bonds, and its total deposits. The bonds in question were usually government bonds issued by the national government.

Financial Profitability focuses on the financial results of banks,

Chapter 5 The Evolution of the Interlocking Directorate Network

most importantly on their return on equity. Some of these are used as mechanisms only in the analysis focusing on the evolution of the network only and are not included in evaluation functions used to analyse behavior and network co – evolution.

- *ROE ego*: this contains the return on equity the bank achieves in the current year.
- *ROE abs difference*: this measures the absolute difference between the ROE of the two partner banks.
- *ROE growth ego*: this contains the absolute growth of the return on equity the bank sees during the current year, so the difference in ROE between two years.
- *ROE growth abs difference*: this variable measures the difference in RoE growth between two banks in the current year.

Network and Behaviour co – evolution

The second part of the analysis focuses on the joint co – evolution of the Interlocking directorate network and the banks' ROE. This requires a change to the mechanisms used to explore the network evolution and the construction of mechanisms for the behaviour evolution.

The first difference is the introduction of a second outcome variable. Due to the constraints of the SIENA methodology it is currently not feasible to use ROE in its continuous form as such. Consequently, I introduce the *ROE band*variable, which categorizes ROE values into 6 bins, each assigned a corresponding value from 1 to 6. The categories are in 5% steps starting at zero with category 6 any ROE value above 25%. The simulations trace how banks change from one bin into others.

The choice of six categories is a compromise between fine ROE gradations to catch any impact and suitability of the data for the simulation. Shifting to a larger number of categories requires simulations to trace banks' movements through a large number of categories within a single period with larger ROE fluctuations, which create substantial problems for the convergence of simulations run. The consequence of larger bins is that the results are much less likely to pick up smaller effects on ROE as they do not necessarily lead to a change in the observed outcome value. As a result of that necessary compromise, the analysis is substantially more suitable for the network side than the behaviour side and the discussion of the results will take that into account.

Besides serving as an additional outcome variable, ROE band is also included as a mechanism explaining the evolution of the interlocking directorate network. Additionally, ROE *band abs difference* is also included. This measures the difference between the ROE band variables of the two banks. When these two mechanisms are included, the variables *ROE ego* and *ROE abs difference* are dropped.

The modelling of the evolution of ROE also requires the inclusion of explanatory mechanisms for this outcome variable. The list of included factors resembles that for the network evolution with those mechanisms removed were based on bank pair characteristics. Consequently, the following mechanisms are used:

• *Linear*: this is the value of the ROE band the bank is currently in.

• *Squared*: this is the square of the value of the ROE band the

Chapter 5 The Evolution of the Interlocking Directorate Network

bank is currently in.

- *Degree*: this is the number of IDs the bank has at that point.
- *Average alter by Alter Assets*: this is the average ROE of all linked banks weighted by the assets of these banks.
- *Bank Opening*: this is the year the bank did open.
- *Log Assets*, *leverage*, *liquidity*, *Bond/Deposits*: these are the same variables as above based on the bank in question.
- *Branches*, *Assets per Executive*: similarly, variables as above based on an individual bank.

5.4 Results

The interpretations of the results differ based on the nature of the outcome, i.e. network or behaviour, and the type of the variable, i.e. monadic or dyadic. In the case of network ties monadic and dyadic variables lead to different effects. A monadic variable, so a characteristic of the tie – initiating bank only, is associated with an effect on all network ties. The resulting value compares the likelihoods to add any tie for two situations where the only difference is in that particular variable for this bank. The result for a dyadic variable, so a variable involving the characteristics of the potential partner, compares the likelihoods for the initiating bank to form that particular tie when the potential partner differs in that particular characteristic only. In the case of behaviour, the effect looks at the likelihood to increase the ROE by one category in comparison the status quo, so remaining in the bank's current category.

5.4.1 Network Development

Table 5.4 (Evolution of the Interlocking Directorate Network) presents the results for the analysis of the network dynamics only, which indicate that there were a number of factors driving the evolution of the interlocking directorate network between modern Chinese banks.

TABLE 5.4 Evolution of the Interlocking Directorate Network

Degree (density)	-1.992	(0.390)	***	-1.659	(0.411)	***
Transitive triads	0.194	(0.027)	***	0.202	(0.025)	***
Distance 2 pairs	-0.001	(0.015)		0.202	(0.025)	
Degree of alter	-0.059	(0.019)	***	-0.049	(0.019)	***
Degree″ (1/2) assortativity	0.096	(0.016)	***	0.089	(0.015)	***
Central Link	0.191	(0.119)		0.261	(0.124)	**
Central Link (period 2)	-0.862	(0.229)	***	-0.767	(0.227)	***
Central Link (period 3)	-0.380	(0.251)		-0.408	(0.261)	
Local Link	0.011	(0.048)		-0.062	(0.054)	
Asset ratio	0.302	(0.098)	***	0.274	(0.100)	***
Co-Location	0.061	(0.054)		0.050	(0.056)	
same Bank Type	0.180	(0.043)	***	0.177	(0.045)	***
Bank age alter	-0.001	(0.005)		-0.003	(0.005)	
Bank age difference	-0.007	(0.004)	*	-0.011	(0.004)	***
Staff alter	0.061	(0.172)		-0.139	(0.191)	
Execs alter	-0.016	(0.009)	*	-0.006	(0.010)	
Branches alter	0.005	(0.004)		0.005	(0.004)	
Asset/Execs alter	0.000	(0.001)		0.001	(0.001)	
log (Assets) alter	0.001	(0.015)		-0.006	(0.016)	

Continued

Leverage alter	0.066	(0.251)		-0.247	(0.289)	
Liquidity alter	0.109	(0.239)		0.182	(0.242)	
Bond. Deposits alter	-0.296	(0.306)		-0.372	(0.341)	
RoE ego				0.028	(0.007)	***
RoE abs. difference				-0.002	(0.001)	**
RoE_growth ego				0.055	(0.008)	***
RoE_growth abs. difference				-0.004	(0.002)	**
rate (period 1)	42.078	(6.926)		33.726	(5.208)	
rate (period 2)	10.594	(0.899)		10.790	(0.999)	
rate (period 3)	22.499	(2.997)		24.343	(2.747)	

Note: Standard errors in parentheses, All variables have a convergence ratio below 0.1.

The symbols ***, **, and * denote significance at the 1%, 5%, and 10% levels, respectively.

ego refers to value of the proposing partner, *alter* I to that of the receiving partner.

In terms of network effects, the degree, so the number of IDs, of both potential partners matter, so the more IDs a bank already had, the less likely it was to add another one. Similarly, the more IDs a bank already had, the less likely it was to be the target of a new partnership. If an ID closed a triad, the bank in question was 22% more likely to be selected as a partner than an otherwise identical bank that did not close a triad. Assortativity indicates that banks prefer a more even distribution of IDs between them.

Geographic proximity of headquarters has a strongly positive, however statistically insignificant effect. Changing the definition of what constitutes the extent of Shanghai, the core financial centre, might however change that. Banks were also 17% more likely to form a partnership with a bank, if that bank is of the same type compared to if it is not but otherwise identical. For example, banks fall into commercial and saving group were 17% more likely to share directors with other commercial and saving banks than otherwise identical farmers and industry banks.

While the actual age did not seem to matter, the age gap did. Banks were actually more likely to form links with banks of a similar age, every year the age gap reduced the likelihood by 1%. The size of bank staffs had a negative effect, though it is very small with 100 additional employees reducing the relative probability by just 3%. In contrast, the number of branch locations had a positive effect with every additional location increasing the relative probability by a percentage point. While the number of executives did not matter, the average size of assets each executive was responsible for, however, mattered.

While the total size of assets seemingly had no direct effect, did the ratio of the assets of the two potential partner banks have an effect. Comparing a 2 : 1 ratio to even size increases the relative probability by about 16%. The level of leverage and liquidity appear to not have had an effect, while banks with a larger investment in securities were less likely to be the target of an interlocking directorate.

The last set of factors concerns the impact of financial profitability in the form of return on equity on the likelihood to form interlocking directorates. The results for ROE and ROE growth indicate that more profitable firms as well as those with a higher profitability growth are forming interlocking directorates faster. The coefficients for the

Chapter 5 The Evolution of the Interlocking Directorate Network

difference between two banks indicate that banks are slightly more likely to form interlocking directorates with other banks that looked like them in terms of profitability.

5.4.2 Network and Performance Co – evolution

The second part of the analysis takes into account the potential endogeneity between interlocking directorates and financial profitability of the banks. As Kong and Ploeckl (2018b) shows, interlocking directorates between Chinese banks were related to an increase in the banks' profits, consequently I extend the analysis to allow for the reciprocal influence of these two characteristics.

This is addressed by including ROE as a second outcome variable. The requirements of the simulation methods are such that the outcome can't be continuous but had to be an ordinal variable. Consequently, ROE is transformed into 6 categories of 5% steps. Each bin is then assigned a discrete integer value, ranging from 1 to 6 in ascending order of ROE. Besides requiring such a particular outcome format, the method also focuses on explaining changes in the outcome variable rather than its level. The simulation results therefore show whether factors are influencing that a bank's ROE moves from one bin into a neighbouring one, so crossing one of the 5% thresholds rather than explaining which bin a bank is in. The small number of bins, however, implies that the method is unlikely to pick up an effect of IDs on ROE if that effect is small in comparison to the 5% step size. Unfortunately, increasing the number of bins substantially creates problems for the estimation procedure, as substantial year to year fluctuations in ROE would require a large amount of changes to be captured by the simulation. Consequently, convergence of the simulation algorithm becomes problematic.

Table 5.5 (Co-evolution of the Interlocking Directorate Network and ROE Levels) contains the results for the analysis. The results for the network component of the analysis are very consistent with those of the network only estimation discussed above. Noticeably, only the level of ROE growth and now the ROE bin mattered, while the differences between two banks no longer have statistically significant effects.

TABLE 5.5 Co-evolution of the Interlocking Directorate Network and ROE Levels

Network Dynamics			
Degree	-2.890	(0.775)	***
Transitive triads	0.258	(0.043)	***
Distance 2 pairs	0.007	(0.033)	
Degree of alter	-0.101	(0.036)	***
Degree" (1/2) assortativity	0.175	(0.026)	
Central Link	0.470	(0.202)	**
Central Link (period 2)	-1.408	(0.402)	***
Central Link (period 3)	-0.605	(0.442)	
Local Link	-0.122	(0.113)	
Asset ratio	0.490	(0.162)	***
Co-location	0.143	(0.099)	
same Bank Type	0.297	(0.080)	***
Bank age alter	-0.004	(0.007)	
Bank age difference	-0.017	(0.007)	**
log_Assets alter	-0.018	(0.030)	
Asset / Exec alter	0.002	(0.002)	

Chapter 5 The Evolution of the Interlocking Directorate Network

Continued

Network Dynamics			
Leverage alter	-0.290	(0.471)	
Liquidity alter	0.374	(0.400)	
Bond. Deposits alter	-0.616	(0.632)	
Staff alter	-0.476	(0.320)	
Execs alter	-0.005	(0.018)	
Branches alter	0.013	(0.006)	**
ROE_band ego	0.275	(0.063)	***
ROE_band difference	-0.014	(0.036)	
ROE growth ego	0.086	(0.025)	***
ROE growth difference	-0.014	(0.020)	
Behaviour Dynamics			
ROE_band linear shape	-0.591	(0.774)	
ROE_band quadratic shape	0.074	(0.039)	*
Degree	-0.000	(0.057)	
av. alters x alter's Assets	-0.553	(1.129)	
Bank age	0.024	(0.011)	**
Branches	-0.022	(0.030)	
Asset / Exec	0.013	(0.013)	
log_Assets	0.031	(0.030)	
Leverage	-0.836	(0.583)	
Liquidity	-0.638	(0.558)	
Bond. Deposits	-2.065	(1.106)	*

Note: Standard errors in parentheses, All variables have a convergence ratio below 0.1.

The symbols ***, **, and * denote significance at the 1%, 5%, and 10% levels, respectively.

ego refers to value of the proposing partner, *alter* I to that of the receiving partner.

The results for the behaviour component, changes in ROE, show that as expected the effect of the number of IDs is statistically insignificant and close to zero. The only statistically signficant effect of other factors are the impact of age, younger banks were more likely to shift to higher ROE bands, while a higher share of investments into bonds was associated with a negative effect, so a shift down into lower bands.

5.5 Conclusion

While there is a large literature on the impact of interlocking directorates, not much attention has been paid to the factors shaping the dynamics of the network itself. This paper does so by in the context of modern Chinese banks during the Nanjing decade of the Chinese republic.

Simulating the evolution of the network reveals that there are a number of effects influencing the formation of links including network effects, such as triads, operational characteristics like the number of branches, financial factors like the ratio of assets of two banks, as well as the financial profitability of a bank. The relevance and impact of these factors confirm that domestic Chinese banks not only formed links based on cliques but clearly also due to business reasons.

An initial attempt is made to illuminate the endogeneity issue between interlocking directorates and bank profitability, though further investigation is necessary to understand whether the found result of no influence of directorates on ROE is due to method

Chapter 5   The Evolution of the Interlocking Directorate Network

constraints or really reflecting the actual economic effect.

The current analysis is a first step in understanding the evolution of the interlocking directorate network. The flexibility of the utilized methodology allows, however, to further by incorporating multiple networks and behaviour outcomes. The main extension possibilities are the inclusion of other linkage networks, in particular social, informal and clique networks as well as individual directors as actors. The evolution of the network can then be analysed not only in reference to the evolution of interlocking directorates between banks but also the careers of individual bankers and their links and relationships.

Chapter 6

Conclusion

One cannot study the remarkable development of Chinese modern banking sector during the Republican Era without understanding the financial elite community, which is distinguished by a culturally specific pattern of networking based on personal relations. The thesis, therefore, focuses on this important part of China's historical financial system, namely Chinese banks created following Western examples, through the lens of board connections, providing a systematic analysis on the structure of the interbank network, its implications regarding corporate decision making as well as economic performance, and the network evolution.

This work contributes to the larger literature in different aspects. First, it advances research on board network. Existing studies of interlocking directorates and their implications have grown in volume (e. g. Ertimur, Ferri, and Maber 2012; Bouwman 2011; Kuang and Lee 2017), however the literature has not yet reached a consensus whether these interlocks are a clear channel for exchanging resources and information among firms[①]. I provide systematic empirical evidence to firmly support that interlocking directorates are useful channels to propagate managerial practices, which change how firms act in an economically and politically risky environment.

Furthermore, my research design improves on prior studies of mechanisms for network contagion. Theoretical research on social influence and peer effects highlights wide implications of social networks for specific topics related to contagion including learning, opinion formation, and financial contagion[②]. In contrast, empirical works in corporate finance on this issue are relatively limited, though Leary and Roberts (2014) identifies whether, how, and why peer firm behavior matters for corporate capital structures; Fracassi (2017) investigates whether managers are influenced by their social peers when making corporate policy decisions. Bouwman (2011) finds that firms interlocked with each other share similar governance

---

[①] For instance, Larcker, So, and Wang (2013) argues that shared directorates between two boards act as channels of information or resource exchange and that better-connected firms end up achieving better economic results. Similar studies look at corporate governance spillover (Bouwman 2011), facilitating investments in corporate innovation (Faleye, Kovacs, and Venkateswaran 2014), and information diffusion (Shropshire 2010). On the other hand, however, the existing literature also highlights several reasons why having a well-connected board may adversely affect firm performance (e. g. Kuang and Lee 2017; Chiu, Teoh, and Tian 2013; Fich and Shivdasani 2006).

[②] Lamberson (2016) and Jackson and Yariv (2011) offer detail surveys on network diffusion and contagion.

practices. My work supplements the network contagion study by exploring the corporate policy diffusion and firm peer effect in a Chinese context, which presents a much cleaner and clearer case to determine the influence of peer institutions that are also direct competitors and peers in a strategic sense. In the Republican Era, banks had close links and often shared directors with each other, ensuring that the shared directors were actively involved in daily operations. In the empirical analysis, I identify policy similarities in a number of strategic policy choices, which provide evidence that the influence was widely pervasive throughout banks' operational decision – making.

Importantly, my research also contributes to our knowledge of the financial history of China. There are limited researches on the development of modern Chinese banks in the precommunist era. Ma (2016), in vanguard work, looks to understand the successful development of the modern Chinese financial sector in Republican China (from year 1911 to year 1937) from an institutional perspective. Sheehan (2005) also adds to the body of literature by highlighting the network of formal and personal relations in the modern domestic banking sector but does not look quantitatively at their impact. Therefore, Sheehan (2005) calls on successive studies to answer to what extent operations and capital holdings followed the structures of interlocking directorships. I contribute to an answer by establishing comprehensive interbanking networks based on shared directors from year 1933 to year 1936, the most critical period in the Nanjing – Decade, and use methods derived from social network analysis (SNA) to show the bank coordination and diffusion of corporate decisions through interlocking directorates.

Additional Information on Chapter 3

A.1 Definitions of Variables

A.1.1 Firm Characteristics

total assets: The total assets of an individual bank. The unit is in Chinese silver dollar (CSD).

ln (assets): Natural logarithm of total assets.

board size: Total number of directors on the board.

#staff: Total number of staff in a bank.

#cities: The number of cities, in which a bank has a branch.

If. connected: A dummy variable indicating whether a bank has a shared director on its board.

est. year: The year, in which the bank was established.

board link strength (BLS): BLS is a proxy to measure the extent of inter-board relations. The value equals the natural logarithm of (1 + number of shared directors) between two firms.

ROE: Return on equity = net profit/shareholder's equity

profit per capita: Profit per capita = net profit/the staff number of an individual bank.

net profit: The actual profit of an individual bank after working expenses not included in the calculation of gross profit have been paid. The unit is in Chinese silver dollar (CSD).

reserve fund: A reserve fund is a savings account or other highly liquid asset set aside by an individual bank to meet any future costs or financial obligations, especially those arising unexpectedly.

deposit all kinds: The sum of deposit of a bank.

loan all kinds: The sum of loan of a bank.

paid in capital: Paid-in capital is the amount of capital "paid in" by investors during common or preferred stock issuances, including the par value of the shares themselves.

cash on hand: Total cash reserve of a bank.

total expenditure: Total expenditure of a bank.

total income: The sum of all money received by an individual bank.

investment in securities: The sum of investment in securities of a bank, including stocks, real estate and government bonds.

fixed assets: Bank assets premises including funiture fixtures.

Appendix A Additional Information on Chapter 3

A. 1. 2 Corporate policy measures

bond. deposit: The ratio of bond value to the total deposit:

$$\frac{bond\ value}{total\ deposit\ of\ individual\ bank}$$

bond. loan: The ratio of bond value to the total loan:

$$\frac{bond\ value}{total\ loan\ of\ individual\ bank}$$

bond. SH: The ratio of bond value to the shareholders' equity:

$$\frac{bond\ value}{shareholders'equity\ of\ individual\ bank}$$

cash. deposit: The ratio of cash reserve to the total deposit of individual bank.

cash. loan: The ratio of cash reserve to the total loan of individual bank.

reserve. loan: The ratio of reserve fund of a bank to its total loan.

reserve. deposit: The ratio of reserve fund of a bank to its total deposit.

A. 1. 3 Bank – pair level controls

agg. dir: The sum of all directors on the board for each bank pair.

diff. dir: The absolute difference between the number of directors of the two banks.

same. type: If the bank pair belongs to the same type.

diff. asset: The natural logarithm of the absolute difference between the assets of the two banks.

diff. RoE: The natural logarithm of the absolute difference between the RoE of the two banks.

agg. staff: The sum of all staff for each bank pair.

diff. staff: The absolute difference between the number of staff of the two banks.

agg. city: The sum of cities in which the bank pair operated.

diff. city: The absolute difference of the number of cities in which the bank pair operated.

same. type: If both banks in pair belong to the same type.

A.2 Network Centrality Measures

I begin with some definitions and terminology that will allow us to talk about network structure and measures of the centrality of nodes in networks. The concept is multidimensional. I focus on two primary dimensions for describing the structure and characteristics of each agent in the network that are central to the social networks literature.

- *Degree*: The degree of a node a is the number of direct connections that involve that node, which is the sum of A's neighborhood in the network. Thus, a node's degree in a network n, denoted as $d_a(n)$, is defined as

$$\deg ree_a(n) \equiv \sum_{a \neq b} g(a,b) \qquad (A.1)$$

where g(a, b) is an indicator that there is a direct link between node a and b. Practically, degree measures how a bank is connected with other firms. A bank may be well – connected if it possesses more channels of communication or resource exchange. Or in the manager network, this measure give us a sense of the social capital/personal connections an individual manager has in the bank sector.

- *Closeness centrality*: The second indicator keeps track of the ease of reaching other nodes. It is defined as the inverse of the average distance between nodes:

$$closeness_i(n) \equiv \frac{(n-1)}{\sum_{i \neq j} l(i,j)} \quad (A.2)$$

where l (i, j) is the the number of connections in the shortest path between two nodes i and j.

A.3 Data Sample on Bank Boards, Directors and Balance Sheets

This part presents excerpts of the data I used in this article from various archives. Figure A.1 is extracted from the annual report of Sin – Hua Trust & Savings Bank, with detailed information on board composition and bank characteristics.

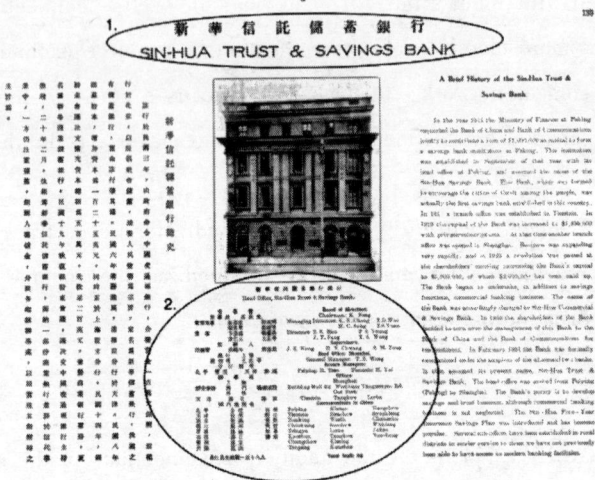

FIGURE A.1　Sample of bank annual introduction with board composition

Notes: The figure presents the annual report front page of Sin‐Hua Trust & Savings Bank (red circle 1), with detailed information on, for example, director list, branch coverage, and total staff numbers (ref circle 2).

Figure A.2 is a screenshot from Modern and Contemporary Persons Integrated Information System—a comprehensive biographical database issued by the Institute of Modern History, Academia Sinica[①]. Figure A.3 shows an example of the balance sheet of the Bank of China 1933 from Economic Research Office (1935, page B 92).

---

① The database is available under http://mhdb.mh.sinica.edu.tw/mhpeople/index.php.

Appendix A Additional Information on Chapter 3

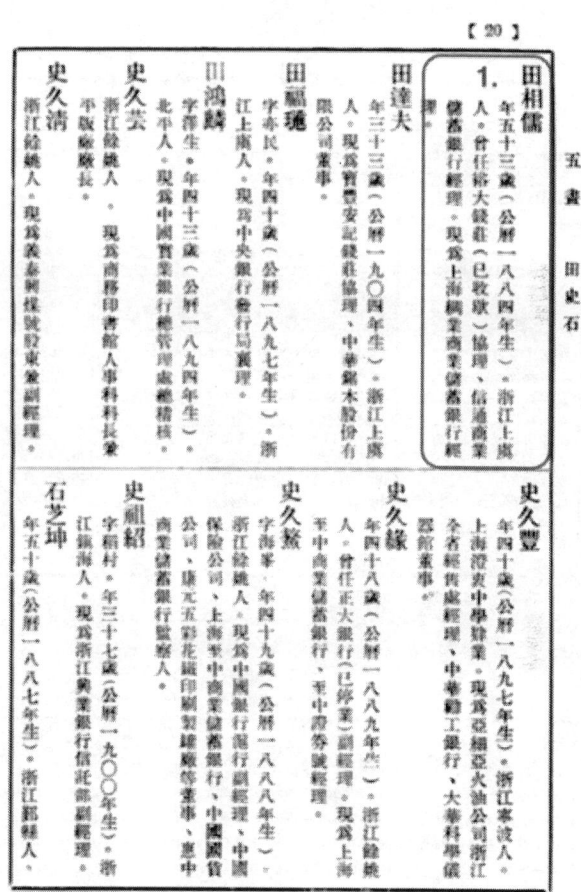

FIGURE A. 2 Sample piece of the biographical database

Notes: The screenshot is extracted from Modern and Contemporary Persons Integrated Information System—a comprehensive biographical database issued by the Institute of Modern History, Academia Sinica. The content in red circle 1 represents a biographical entry, in which one finds the name, age, birthplace, and employment chronicle.

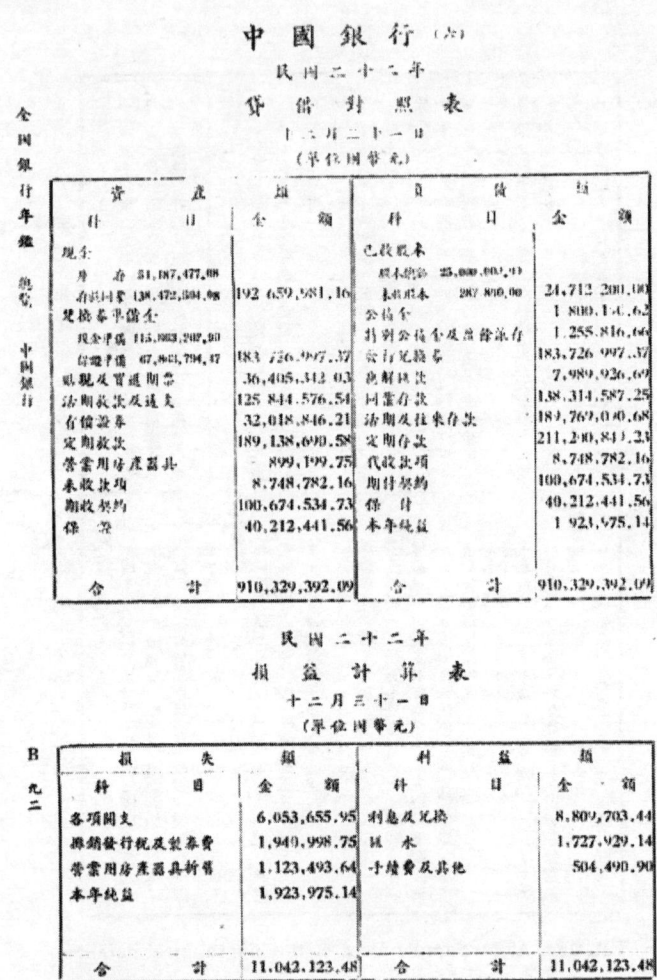

FIGURE A.3 Screenshot of the balance sheet of the Bank of China in 1933

Notes: The figure shows an example of the balance sheet of the Bank of China 1933 from Economic Research Office (1935, page B 92).

Additional Information on Chapter 4

B.1 Variable Definitions

ROA: Return on assets = net profit/total assets

profit per capita: Profit per capita = net profit/the staff number of an individual bank.

assets: The total assets of an individual bank. The unit is in Chinese silver dollar (CSD).

#board members: Total number of directors on the board.

#city: The number of cities, in which a bank has a branch.

age: The age of an individual bank.

#staff: Total number of staff in a bank.

liquidity: An indicator to measure how much liquid assets of a bank possess. *liquidity* = (*reserve fund* + *cash on hand*)/*deposits all kind*.

investment in securities: The sum of investment in securities of a bank, including stocks, real estate and government bonds.

leverage: *leverage = (deposits all kind)/total assets.*

D/S ratio: D/S ratio = #board members/#staff.

B.2 Network Centrality Measures

We begin with some definitions and terminology that will allow us to talk about network structure and measures of the centrality of nodes in networks. The concept is multidimensional. We focus on four primary dimensions of describing the structure and characteristics of each agent in the network that are central to the social networks literature.

- *Degree*: The degree of a node a is the number of direct connections that involve that node, which is the sum of A's neighborhood in the network. Thus, a node a's degree in a network n, denoted as $d_a(n)$, is defined as

$$\deg ree_a(n) \equiv \sum_{a \neq b} g(a,b) \qquad (B.1)$$

where g(a, b) is an indicator that there is a direct link between node a and b. Practically, degree measures how a bank connected with other firms. A bank may be well-connected if it possesses more channels of communications or resource exchange. Or in the manager network, this measure give us a sense of the social capital/personal connections an individual manager own in the bank sector.

- *Closeness centrality*: The second indicator keeps track of the

Appendix B Additional Information on Chapter 4

ease of reaching other nodes. It is defined as the inverse of the average distance between nodes:

$$closeness_i(n) \equiv \frac{(n-1)}{\sum_{i \neq j} l(i,j)} \qquad (B.2)$$

where l (i, j) is the the number of connections in the shortest path between two nodes i and j.

- *Betweenness centrality*: This measure describes the role of a node as an intermediary in the network. For instance, It shows us the average proportion of paths between two outside banks on which a bank lies in the inter-bank network and represents how important a firm is in connecting other ones to each other. It was first proposed by Freeman (1977). Mathematically, the betweenness centrality of a node i is

$$betweenness_i(n) \equiv \sum_{k \neq j; i \in |k,j|} \frac{P_i(kj)/P(kj)}{(n-1)(n-2)/2} \qquad (B.3)$$

letting P_i (k, j) denote the total number of shortest paths between nodes k and j that i lies on and P (k, j) denotes the total numbers of shortest paths between nodes k and j. If this indicator close to 1, that means i lies on most of the shortest paths linking k to j, while the node i is less significant if it is close to 0.

- *Eigenvector centrality*: This network indicator elucidates that having more direct connections is more influential when such connection can reach more nodes, i.e. a bank/manager is well-connected when its direct contracts are also well-connected, or as the motto: "Not what you know, but who you know." Eigenvector centrality measures the importance of the node i in a way that

$$\lambda \cdot centrality_i = \sum_j g_{ij} \cdot centrality_j \qquad (B.4)$$

where λ is the proportion factor and $g_{ij} = 1$ if banks i and j are connected. One can convert equation B. 4 into vector form, then we see:

$$\lambda \cdot Eigenvector = G \cdot Eigenvector \qquad (B.5)$$

where G is a matrix known as adjacency matrix, in which contains element g_{ij} in position (i, j), and it equals 1 if nodes i and j are linked or 0 otherwise. This indicator often demonstrates power or prestige of a node in social network, since the centrality captured is proportional to the sum of neighbor's centralities.

B. 3　Representing and Measuring Networks

We use various measures and methods from network theory to present the network structure. Among them, some terminologies are particularly important to understand the network pattern.

A component in the network is a subset of the network that its vertexes are interconnected. In contrast, isolated directors, which have been mentioned in the main text, are those nodes, which have no connections to other directors in the network. Average path length indicates the average shortest number of steps among two arbitrary directors (nodes). Diameter is an indicator shows the longest number of steps between any two nodes in the network, and clustering coefficient describes an enumeration of the proportion of vertex triples that form triangles, i. e. , all three nodes pairs are connected by edges.

For a further understanding regarding representing and measuring Networks, please refer to Jackson (2010, Chap. 2).

Appendix B Additional Information on Chapter 4

B. 4 A Propensity – Score Matching (PSM) Analysis of the Difference in Performance Between Connected and Isolated Banks

To better neutralize the effects of bank characteristic from two groups of our difference – in – means test in section 4.4.1, we introduce a propensity score matching based on the principal characteristics of banks (i. e. the size of the bank, total operational years, business covered cities, and total staff numbers) in the first stage probability model. Table B.1 demonstrates the sample size after matching. The number of connected banks, as control group, declines from 344 to 127 to match the treated group (banks without busy directors).

TABLE B.1 Sample size summary after matching

	Control	Treated
All	344	127
Matched	127	127
Unmatched	217	0
Discarded	0	0

Figure B.1 highlights the estimated probability densities of matched and unmatched units cross the sample. The overlapping assumption of the propensity score matching analysis is most valid.

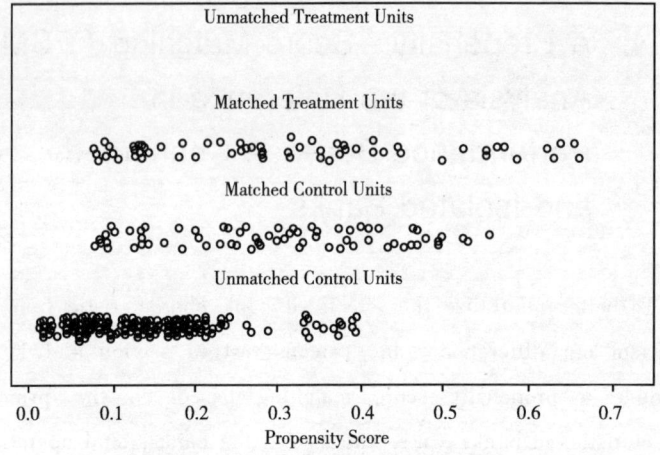

FIGURE B.1　Distribution of propensity scores

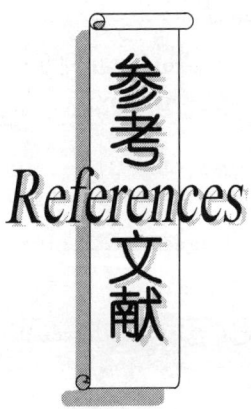

References

Acheson, Graeme G et al. (2016a). "Corporate Ownership, Control and Firm Performance in Victorian Britain". In: Journal of Economic History 76.1, pp. 1 –40.

Anjos, Fernando and Cesare Fracassi (2015). "Shopping for Information? Diversification and the Network of Industries". In: Management Science 61.1, pp. 161 –183.

Bakhshandeh, Reza et al. (2011). "Degrees of separation in social networks". In: Fourth Annual Symposium on Combinatorial Search.

Balland, Pierre – Alexandre, Mathijs De Vaan, and Ron Boschma (2012). "The dynamics of interfirm networks along the industry life cycle: The case of the global video game industry, 1987 – 2007". In: Journal of Economic Geography 13.5, pp. 741 –765.

Bergere, Marie – Claire (1989). Golden Age of the Chinese

Bourgeoisie, 1911 – 1937. Cambridge University Press.

Bizjak, John, Michael Lemmon, and Ryan Whitby (2009). "Option backdating and board interlocks". In: The Review of Financial Studies 22.11, pp. 4821 – 4847.

Block, Per and Thomas Grund (2014). "Multidimensional homophily in friendship networks". In: Network Science 2.2, pp. 189 – 212.

Bonavia, David (1995). China's warlords. Oxford University Press, USA.

Borgatti, Stephen P and Pacey C Foster (2003). "The network paradigm in organizational research: A review and typology". In: Journal of management 29.6, pp. 991 – 1013.

Bouwman, Christa HS (2011). "Corporate governance propagation through overlapping directors". In: The Review of Financial Studies 24.7, pp. 2358 – 2394.

Braggion, Fabio (2011). "Managers and (secret) social networks: The influence of the freemasonry on firm performance". In: Journal of the European Economic Association 9.6, pp. 1053 – 1081.

Braggion, Fabio, Alberto Manconi, and Haikun Zhu (2018). "Credit and Social Unrest: Evidence from 1930s China". In: Available at SSRN 2714815.

Brayshay, Mark, Mark Cleary, and John Selwood (2007). "Social networks and the transnational reach of the corporate class in the early – twentieth century". In: Journal o/Historical Geography 33.1, pp. 144 – 167.

Campbell, Gareth and John D Turner (2011). "Substitutes for legal protection: corporate governance and dividends in Victorian

Britain". In: The Economic History Review 64. 2, pp. 571 – 597.

Cheadle, Jacob E et al. (2013). "The differential contributions of teen drinking homophily to new and existing friendships: An empirical assessment of assortative and proximity selection mechanisms". In: Social science research 42. 5, pp. 1297 – 1310.

Cheng, Linsun (2003). Banking in modern China: entrepreneurs, professional managers, and the development o/ Chinese banks, 1897 – 1937. Cambridge University Press.

Chiu, Peng Chia, Siew Hong Teoh, and Feng Tian (2013). "Board Interlocks and Earnings Management Contagion". In: The Accounting Review 88. 3, pp. 915 – 944.

Coble, Parks M (1986). The Shanghai Capitalists and the Nationalist Government, 1927 – 1937. 94. Harvard Univ Asia Center.

Colvin, Christopher L, Abe de Jong, and Philip T Fliers (2015). "Predicting the past: Understanding the causes of bank distress in the Netherlands in the 1920s". In: Explorations in Economic History 55, pp. 97 – 121.

Dass, Nishant et al. (2014). "Board Expertise: Do Directors from Related Industries Help Bridge the Information Gap?" In: Review o/Financial Studies 27. 5, pp. 1533 – 1592.

Deloof, Marc and Veronique Vermoesen (2016). "The value of corporate boards during the Great Depression in Belgium". In: Explorations in Economic History 62, pp. 108 – 123.

Eastman, Lloyd E et al. (1991). The Nationalist Era in China, 1927 – 1949. Cambridge University Press.

Economic Research Office General Management Office, Bank of China (1935). Quanguo yinhang nianjian 1935 [BankAnnual 1935]. Shanghai.

— (1936). Quanguo yinhang nianjian 1936 [Bank Annual 1936]. Shanghai.

— (1937). Quanguo yinhang nianjian 1937 [Bank Annual 1937]. Shanghai.

El-Khatib, Rwan, Kathy Fogel, and Tomas Jandik (2015). "CEO network centrality and merger performance". In: Journal of Financial Economics 116.2, pp. 349-382.

Ertimur, Yonca, Fabrizio Ferri, and David A Maber (2012). "Reputation penalties for poor monitoring of executive pay: Evidence from option backdating". In: Journal of Financial Economics 104.1, pp. 118-144.

Esteves, R and F Ploeckl (2016). Gold and Trade: An Empirical Simulation Approach. Tech. rep. q Mimeo.

Fairbank, J.K. (1978). The Cambridge History of China: Volume 10, Late Ch'ing 1800-1911. The Cambridge History of China pt. 1. Cambridge University Press.

Fairbank, J.K. and K.C. Liu (1980). The Cambridge History of China: Volume 11, Late Ch'ing, 1800-1911. The Cambridge History of China pt. 2. Cambridge University Press.

Faleye, Olubunmi, Tunde Kovacs, and Anand Venkateswaran (2014). "Do Better-Connected CEOs Innovate More?" In: Journal of Financial and Quantitative Analysis 49.5-6, pp. 1201-1225.

Fewsmith, Joseph (1985). Party, State, and Local Elites in Republican China: Merchant Organizations and Politics in Shanghai,

1890 – 1930. Univ of Hawaii Pr.

Fich, Eliezer M and Anil Shivdasani (2006). "Are busy boards effective monitors?" In: The Journal of finance 61. 2, pp. 689 – 724.

Field, Laura, Michelle Lowry, and Anahit Mkrtchyan (2013). "Are busy boards detrimental?" In: Journal ofFinancial Economics 109. 1, pp. 63 – 82.

Fracassi, Cesare (2017). "Corporate Finance Policies and Social Networks". In: Management Science 63. 8, pp. 2420 – 2438.

Fracassi, Cesare and Geoffrey Tate (2012). "External Networking and Internal Firm Governance". In: The Journal of Finance 67. 1, pp. 153 – 194.

Freeman, Linton C (1977). "A set of measures of centrality based on betweenness". In: Sociometry, pp. 35 – 41.

Gao, P et al. (2012). "Friends with money". In: Journal of Financial Economics 103. 1, pp. 169 – 188.

Giulietti, Corrado, Jackline Wahba, and Yves Zenou (2018). "Strong versus weak ties in migration". In: European Economic Review 104, pp. 111 – 137.

Granovetter, Mark (1985). "Economic action and social structure: The problem of embeddedness". In: American journal of sociology 91. 3, pp. 481 – 510.

Granovetter, Mark S (1977). "The strength of weak ties". In: Social networks. Elsevier, pp. 347 – 367.

Gurevitch, Michael (1961). "The social structure of acquaintanceship networks". PhD thesis. Massachusetts Institute of Technology.

Hackbarth, Dirk (2008). "Managerial traits and capital

structure decisions". In: Journal of Financial and Quantitative Analysis 43.4, pp. 843 – 881.

Haselmann, Rainer, David Schoenherr, and Vikrant Vig (2018). "Rent seeking in elite networks". In: Journal of Political Economy 126.4, pp. 1638 – 1690.

Haunschild, Pamela R and Christine M Beckman (1998). "When Do Interlocks Matter?: Alternate Sources of Information and Interlock Influence". In: Administrative Science Quarterly 43.4, p. 815.

Helmers, Christian, Manasa Patnam, and P Raghavendra Rau (2017). "Do board interlocks increase innovation? Evidence from a corporate governance reform in India". In: Journal of Banking & Finance 80, pp. 51 – 70.

Ho, Chun – Yu and Dan Li (2013). "A mirror of history: China's bond market, 1921 – 42". In: The Economic History Review 67.2, pp. 409 – 434.

Hochberg, Yael V, Alexander Ljungqvist, and Yang Lu (2007). "Whom you know matters: Venture capital networks and investment performance". In: The Journal of Finance 62.1, pp. 251 – 301.

Holmes, Simon C, and Florian Ploeckl (2014). "Bank on steel? Joint – stock banks and the rationalization of the British interwar steel industry". In: European Review of Economic History 19.1, pp. 88 – 107.

— (2009). "Networks and Economic Behavior". In: Annual Review of Economics 1.1, pp. 489 – 511.

— (2010). Social and economic networks. Princeton university press.

— (2014). "Networks in the Understanding of Economic Behaviors". In: Journal of Economic Perspectives 28.4, pp. 3-22.

Jackson, Matthew O, Brian W Rogers, and Yves Zenou (2016). "The economic consequences of social network structure". In: Available at SSRN 2467812.

— (2017). "The Economic Consequences of Social - Network Structure". In: Journal of Economic Literature 55.1, pp. 49-95.

Jackson, Matthew O. and Leeat Yariv (2011). "Diffusion, strategic interaction, and social structure". In: Handbook of social Economics. Vol. 1. Elsevier, pp. 645-678.

Jackson, Matthew O. et al. (2008). Social and economic networks. Vol. 3. Princeton University Press Princeton.

Ji, Zhaojin (2003). A History of Modern Shanghai Banking: The Rise and Decline of China's Finance Capitalism. ME Sharpe.

Kang, Eugene (2008). "Director Interlocks and Spillover Effects of Reputational Penalties from Financial Reporting Fraud". In: The Academy of Management Journal 51.3, pp. 537-555.

Kong, Lingyu (2018). "Corporate policies propagation throughboard connections: Evidence from modern Chinese banking in the 1930s". In: The University of Adelaide, School of Economics, working paper series.

Kong, Lingyu and Florian Ploeckl (2018a). "Building a Web of Connections: The Evolution of the Interlocking Directorate Network of modern Chinese Banks in the Republican Era". In: The University of Adelaide, School of Economics, working paper series.

— (2018b). "Connections and Performance: The Impact of Interlocking Directorates on modern Chinese banks in the Republican

Era". In: The University of Adelaide, School of Economics, working paper series.

— (2018c). "Modern Chinese Banking Networks during the Republican Era". In: The University of Adelaide, School of Economics, working paper series.

Kuang, Yu Flora and Gladys Lee (2017). "Corporate fraud and external social connectedness of independent directors". In: Journal of Corporate Finance 45, pp. 401 – 427.

Lamberson, PJ (2016). "Diffusion in networks". In: The Oxford Handbook of the Economics of Networks.

Lan, R. (2014). Transformation of China's Modern Banking System: From the Late Qing Era to the 1930s. The Transformation of China's Banking System from the Late Qing Era to The 1930s Series. Enrich Professional Publishing. ISBN: 9781623200800.

Lan, R. (2015). Transformation of China's Modern Banking System: From the Late Qing Era to the 1930s. Transformation of China's Modern Banking System: From the Late Qing Era to the 1930s v. 1. Enrich Professional Publishing. ISBN: 9781623200800.

Larcker, David F, Eric C So, and Charles CY Wang (2013). "Boardroom centrality and firm performance". In: Journal of Accounting and Economics 55.2, pp. 225 – 250.

Leary, Mark T and Michael R Roberts (2014). "Do Peer Firms Affect Corporate Financial Policy?" In: The Journal of Finance 69.1, pp. 139 – 178.

Luke, Douglas A (2015). A user's guide to network analysis in R. Springer.

Manger, Mark S and Mark A Pickup (2016). "The coevolution

of trade agreement networks and democracy". In: Journal of Conflict Resolution 60.1, pp. 164 – 191.

Mariolis, Peter (1975). "Interlocking directorates and control of corporations: The theory of bank control". In: Social Science Quarterly, pp. 425 – 439.

McConnell, John J and Henri Servaes (1990). "Additional evidence on equity ownership and corporate value". In: Journal of Financial economics 27.2, pp. 595 – 612.

Mizruchi, Mark S (1989). "Similarity of political behavior among large American corporations". In: American Journal of Sociology 95.2, pp. 401 – 424.

Mol, Michael J (2001). "Creating wealth through working with others: Interorganizational relationships". In: Academy of Management Perspectives 15.1, pp. 150 – 152.

Myers, Stewart C (2001). "Capital structure". In: Journal of Economic perspectives 15.2, pp. 81 – 102.

Nguyen, Duc Duy, Jens Hagendorff, and Arman Eshraghi (2015). "Can bank boards prevent misconduct?" In: Review of Finance, rfv011.

Nishimura, Shizuya (2005). "The foreign and native banks in China: Chop loans in Shanghai and Hankow before 1914". In: Modern Asian Studies 39.1, pp. 109 – 132.

Okumura, Tetsu (1979). "Kyoko Ka Kosetsu Sanshigyo no Saihen". In: (Restructuring of the Jiangsu and Zhejiang silk industry under the Great Depression), Toyoshi Kenkyu 37, pp. 80 – 116.

Padgett, John F and Christopher K Ansell (1993). "Robust Action and the Rise of the Medici, 1400 – 1434". In: American journal of sociology, pp. 1259 – 1319.

Parker, A and R Cross (2004). "The Hidden Power of Social Networks". In: pp. 3 – 31 – 91 – 109.

Patacchini, Eleonora and Yves Zenou (2008). "The strength of weak ties in crime". In: European Economic Review 52.2, pp. 209 – 236.

Rawski, T G (1989). Economic Growth in Prewar China. University of California Press.

Ren, Bing, Kevin Y Au, and Thomas A Birtch (2009). "China's business network structure during institutional transitions". In: Asia Pacific Journal of Management 26.2, pp. 219 – 240.

Renneboog, Luc and Yang Zhao (2014). "Director networks and takeovers". In: Journal of Corporate Finance 28, pp. 218 – 234.

Rinaldi, Alberto and Michelangelo Vasta (2005). "The structure of Italian capitalism, 1952 – 1972: new evidence using the interlocking directorates technique". In: Financial History Review 12.02, pp. 173 – 226.

Robb, Alicia M and David T Robinson (2014). "The capital structure decisions of new firms". In: The Review of Financial Studies 27.1, pp. 153 – 179.

Rousseau, Peter L and Caleb Stroup (2015). "Director histories and the pattern of acquisitions". In: Journal of Financial and Quantitative Analysis 50.4, pp. 671 – 698.

Sheehan, Brett (2005). "Myth and reality in Chinese financial cliques in 1936". In: Enterprise & Society 6.3, pp. 452 – 491.

Shiroyama, Tomoko (2008). China during the Great Depression:

market, state, and the world economy, 1929 - 1937. Vol. 294. Harvard Univ Council on East Asian.

Shropshire, Christine (2010). "The role of the interlocking director and board receptivity in the diffusion of practices". In: Academy of Management Review 35.2, pp. 246 - 264.

Shue, Kelly (2013). "Executive networks and firm policies: Evidence from the random assignment of MBA peers". In: The Review of Financial Studies 26.6, pp. 1401 - 1442.

Snijders, Tom AB, Gerhard G Van de Bunt, and Christian EG Steglich (2010). "Introduction to stochastic actor - based models for network dynamics". In: Social networks 32.1, pp. 44 - 60.

Steglich, Christian, Tom AB, and Michael Pearson (2010). "Dynamic Networks and Behavior: Separating Selection from Influence". In: Sociological methodology 40.1, pp. 329 - 393.

Tamagna, Frank M (1942). Banking and finance in China. International Secretariat, Institute of Pacific Relations.

Tong - na, Chang (2014). "Impact of location choice of branches of modern Chinese banks on their performance". In: Journal of finance and economics (in Chinese) 40.2, pp. 120 - 132.

Topa, Giorgio (2011). "Labor markets and referrals". In: Handbook of social economics. Vol. 1. Elsevier, pp. 1193 - 1221.

Travers, Jeffrey and Stanley Milgram (1967). "The small world problem". In: Phychology Today 1, pp. 61 - 67.

— (1969). "An experimental study of the small world problem". In: Sociometry, pp. 425 - 443.

Wang, Yeh - chien (1981). "The Development of Money and Banking in Modern China, 1644 - 1937". In: Taibei: Institute of

Economics, Academia Sinica, 1981. Yang, Lien - sheng.

Westphal, James D, Marc - David L Seidel, and Katherine J Stewart (2001). "Second - order imitation: Uncovering latent effects of board network ties". In: Administrative Science Quarterly 46.4, pp. 717 - 747.

Wilson, John F, Emily Buchnea, and Anna Tilba (2017). "The British corporate network, 1904 - 1976: Revisiting the finance - industry relationship". In: Business History, pp. 1 - 28.

Withers, Michael, Ji Youn Rose Kim, and Michael Howard (2018). "The evolution of the board interlock network following Sarbanes - Oxley". In: Social Networks 52, pp. 56 - 67.

Xin, Katherine K and Jone L Pearce (1996). "Guanxi: Connections as substitutes for formal institutional support". In: Academy of management journal 39.6, pp. 1641 - 1658.

XU, Mao, Guanlin GU, and Tianying JIANG (1997). Zhong guo shi yin hang jia, Top ten bankers in China (in translation).

Xu, Xiaoqun (2000). Chinese professionals and the republican state: The rise of professional associations in Shanghai, 1912 - 1937. Cambridge University Press.

Young, A N (1971). China's nation - building effort, 1927 - 1937: the financial and economic record. Hoover press publications. Hoover Institution Press.

Zhaojin, Ji (2016). A history of modern Shanghai banking: The rise and decline of China's financial capitalism. Routledge.